Penguin Books

The Continuum Concept

Jean Liedloff was born and brought up in New York. She graduated from Drew Seminary for Young Women and went on to Cornell University, but began her travels without taking a degree. Attracted to Europe, then to the South American jungle, she made four expeditions among the Stone Age Indians of Venezuela before becoming convinced that 'we in Western civilization have tragically misunderstood our own nature.' After a fifth expedition that confirmed her retrospective observations, she wrote *The Continuum Concept*.

Jean Liedloff has written for the *Sunday Times* and was a founding editor of the *Ecologist* magazine. She now lectures and broadcasts around the world to students, doctors, parents, psychotherapists and a general public looking for explanations and remedies for personal alienation and social ills. Jean Liedloff lives in London where she practises and teaches psychotherapy based on the principles of *The Continuum Concept*. She is planning books on this work and on the rearing of children without conflict. *The Continuum Concept* has received great critical acclaim and has earned a substantial following in many countries.

The *Sunday Telegraph* said, 'It is really a thesis about achieving fulfilment. It is time we reappraised ourselves and discovered what sort of animal we are. We have a standard of living while the Yequana have a quality of life.'

Dr Frances Ilg, author of *Infant and Child* and eminent pediatrician at the Gesell Institute in New Haven, Connecticut, said, 'It is a most remarkable book ... We have especially met resistance from parents. Something tells me they will listen to this.'

Frankfurter Allgemeine called it 'inspiring and informative'.

Psychologie Heute said it is 'The rare case of an optimistic radical book. It shakes the foundations of our conceptions without razing them to the ground, rather a catalyst than dynamite, with a lasting effect on everyday life,' and selected it as one of The Year's Best Books.

The *Sunday Telegraph Magazine* wrote, 'Miss Liedloff writes beautifully, never stooping to jargon, and her own personal involvement gives her story an immediacy that is most moving.'

Jean Liedloff

The Continuum Concept

Penguin Books

PENGUIN BOOKS

Published by the Penguin Group
27 Wrights Lane, London w8 5tz, England
Viking Penguin Inc., 40 West 23rd Street, New York, New York 10010, USA
Penguin Books Australia Ltd, Ringwood, Victoria, Australia
Penguin Books Canada Ltd, 2801 John Street, Markham, Ontario, Canada l3r 1b4
Penguin Books (NZ) Ltd, 182–190 Wairau Road, Auckland 10, New Zealand

Penguin Books Ltd, Registered Offices: Harmondsworth, Middlesex, England

First published by Duckworth 1975
Published in paperback by Futura 1976
Revised edition published in Penguin Books 1986
10 9 8 7 6 5 4

Made and printed in Great Britain by
Richard Clay Ltd, Bungay, Suffolk
Typeset in Monophoto Photina

For Adam Yarmolinsky, Jonathan Miller, John Horder, Jonas Salk, Tarzie Vittachi and David Hearn who, when they understood the concept, took responsibility upon themselves for its furtherance, just as I had. And for Mouse and Janet with love.

Contents

steps away from the state of grace: man's evolved ability to make an intellectual choice and civilized man's derailment from the continuum / Relief from thinking, meditation, ritual and other thought-erasers

Some Reports and Thoughts for the Second Edition

On Parents

Three months before this book was first published in 1975, a friend asked me to lend my proof copy to a couple who were expecting their first baby. I met Millicent, the wife, later when she came to lunch with Seth, who was by then three months old. She told me that she and her doctor husband, Mark, were convinced that my ideas made sense because they corresponded to their own feelings. She was very keen that other parents read the book but was worried that some might be discouraged by the idea that they had to carry the baby about constantly for months.

'I could see the point,' she said, 'but I was sure I was not going to lug the equivalent of a ten- or fifteen-pound sack of potatoes around all day and night. I'm afraid you might put people off altogether. Why don't you just stick to "Put the shopping in the pram and carry the baby", as I heard you say on the radio? Most of them will probably be willing to do that, and when they get home they'll want to go on carrying it. I never did put Seth down because I didn't feel like it.'

'That was the idea,' I said. 'It's only when the baby is there and *your* feelings for it are not negated that it works, not because someone said you should. Nor would you be likely to want to be stuck in the service of just "*a* baby" to that extent before you had met and fallen in love with it.'

'I solved the problem of my bath by taking Seth in with me and bathing him at the same time,' she went on. 'If Mark gets home in time, he can't resist jumping in too. He loves sleeping with Seth as much as I do.

'I've found ways to do all my housework and gardening without putting Seth down. I put him down only when I'm making a bed and bounce him around among the sheets and blankets, and he loves that. And I do wait until Mark can help me bring the coal up from the basement. The only time Seth and I are separated is when I'm riding my horse. A friend holds him then. But I'm always eager to take him back at the end of the ride. It feels right to have him with me. Luckily, I have a printing business with a friend, so I didn't have to give up my job. I work standing up, and by now I'm used to having him in a sling on my back or hip. I can swing him around to the front if he wants to feed. He doesn't have to cry; he just grunts and reaches. At night too he only has to nuzzle about and I know he's hungry. I just plug in a bosom and don't even really have to wake up.'

Seth was relaxed and quiet through lunch and, like a Yequana baby, no trouble to hold.

It is understandable that Western babies are not welcome in offices, shops, workrooms or even at dinner parties. They usually shriek and kick, wave their arms and stiffen their bodies, so that one needs two hands, and a lot of attention, to keep them under control. It seems that they are keyed up with undischarged energy as a result of spending so much time out of contact with an active person's naturally discharging energy field that, when they are picked up, they are still rigid with tension and try to rid themselves of the discomfort by flexing their limbs or signalling the person holding them to bounce them on a knee or throw them up in the air and catch them. Millicent was surprised at the difference between Seth's soft body tone and that of other babies. She said they all felt like pokers.

As soon as it is recognized that treating babies as we did for hundreds of thousands of years assures us of calm, soft, undemanding little creatures, they need no longer cause conflict in working mothers who are unwilling to be bored and isolated all day with no adult companionship. The babies would be where they need to be, with their mothers at work; and the mothers would be where they need to be, with their peers, doing not baby care but something worthy of an intelligent adult. But employers are not likely to be receptive until the reputation of babies has improved. *Ms* magazine made a heroic effort to bring babies into their office, but it need not have been so heroic if the babies had not been isolated in carriers on nearby desks but had been in physical contact with someone instead.

Not everyone puts continuum principles into practice as early and as happily as Millicent and Mark, who now have more children brought up like Seth. One mother, Anthea, wrote to me that as soon as she read the book she realized she should have listened to her instincts instead of the babycare 'experts', but now she had a four-year-old, Trevor, to whom she had done 'all the wrong things'. Another baby was on its way and would be a 'continuum baby' from the start, but what to do about Trevor?

Not only is it difficult to carry a four-year-old about to make up his lost in-arms stage, but it is also important for him to play and explore and learn as befits his chronological age. I suggested that Anthea and Brian take Trevor to sleep with them at night and leave things pretty much as they were in the daytime, except for welcoming the boy on their laps and being physically available to him whenever possible. I also asked them to keep a daily record of what happened, as it was soon after the book had come out and I thought their experience might be useful to others.

Anthea kept the record faithfully. For the first few nights none of them had much sleep. Trevor would wriggle and whine. There were toes up noses, elbows in ears. Glasses of water were called for at ungodly hours. Once Trevor jockeyed himself into a position perpendicular, instead of parallel, to his parents, resulting in their clinging to the edges of the mattress on either side. More than once Brian stomped off to his office in the morning red-eyed and irritable. But they persevered, unlike others who would say to me, after three or four trial nights, 'It doesn't work; we couldn't sleep,' and give up.

After three months, Anthea reported, there were no more disturbances; all three slept blissfully through the nights. And not only did the relationships of Anthea with Trevor and Brian with Trevor improve markedly, but so did Anthea's and Brian's. 'And,' she said at the end of her report, mentioning the topic for the first time, 'Trevor stopped being aggressive at school!'

Trevor moved back to his own bed some months later of his own accord, having had his fill of what would have been infant sleeping experience. His new sister was, of course, in their parents' bed too, and even after he had moved on Trevor knew he was welcome there whenever he felt the need.

It was reassuring to know that, after four years, one could

accomplish so much repair work in only three months. I was most heartened and able to tell Trevor's story to lecture audiences and people who wrote to me with like questions thenceforward.

Why not to Feel Guilty about not having been the Only One
in Western Civilization to Treat your Child Correctly

Another lady, Rachel, whose family of four was half-grown, wrote, 'I think your book was one of the cruellest things I've ever read. I am not suggesting that you should not have written it. I am not even saying that I wish I had not read it. It's simply that it impressed me profoundly, hurt me deeply, intrigued me greatly. I do not want to face the possible truth of your theory and am trying my best to avoid facing it ... (God forgive you for that sequence about what babies go through, by the way, because, in the deathless words of Noël Coward, I never shall!) ... It's a wonder to me, as a matter of fact, that you were not tarred and feathered at some stage ... Every mother who reads it must do everything she can to avoid its implications ... Do you know, I honestly believe that it was only while I thought that all the aggravation we go through was normal and unavoidable – "natural!" to use a word one often hears by way of comfort from other mothers, child psychologists and books – that it was endurable at all. Now that you have intruded into my mind the idea that it could be otherwise, well, I don't mind telling you that for twenty-four hours after reading your book, not to mention during, I was so depressed I felt like shooting myself.'

Happily, she did not, and we have since become close friends, she a great advocate of the continuum concept and I a great admirer of her honesty and her way with words. But the sentiments she expressed, the depression, the guilt, the regret, have occurred all too often among readers with grown children.

Yes, of course, it is dreadful to think what we have done, with the best of intentions, to the people we most love. Let us think too of what our loving parents have equally ignorantly/innocently done to us and what was undoubtedly done to them. Most of the literate world joins us in the victimization of each new, trusting babe. It has become our custom (for reasons I shall not speculate on here). Does any one of us, therefore, have the right to take the guilt, or even the awful sense of having been cheated, upon herself or himself, as though one alone could have known better?

On the other hand, if, fearing that unreasonable sense of personal guilt, we refuse to acknowledge what is being done to all of us by all of us, then how can we hope to change any part of it? The part nearest us, for example? Nancy, a beautiful, white-haired lady at a lecture of mine in London, said that since she and her thirty-five-year-old daughter had both read my book, their understanding of their relationship had brought them closer together than they had ever been before. Another mother, Rosalind, told me how she had sunk into a weeping depression for several days after reading the book. Her husband was understanding and patiently took care of their two little girls while Rosalind languished, unable to continue her life in the new light. 'At a certain point,' she told me, 'I realized that my only way ahead was to read the book again ... this time for strength.'

On Our Strange Inability to See

An acquaintance telephoned me one day in a state of great excitement because he had been seated in a bus behind a West Indian lady with a small child who were enjoying an easy, respectful relationship of a sort seldom seen in British society. 'It was beautiful,' he said. 'I had just finished reading your book and there they were, living illustrations. I've been among lots of people like them before without ever seeing what now seems so obvious. I certainly never appreciated the lesson they could be to us if we could understand how they got that way ... and why we never do.'

So blind are we that there is actually an organization in Britain called the National Association for Parents of Sleepless Children. Apparently it functions on the model of Alcoholics Anonymous, fortifying the victims of screaming babies with sympathy from fellow sufferers and consolations like, 'They do outgrow it eventually', 'Take turns with your spouse so that each of you can sleep sometimes while the other gets up', 'It won't hurt a baby to be left to cry if you know there is nothing wrong with it.' The best they have to say is, 'If everything else fails, it won't really do the baby any harm to let it sleep in your bed.'

There is never a suggestion that they might call off the war and believe the babies, who unanimously, and perfectly clearly, let everyone know where a baby's place is.

On Being 'Child-centred' or Permissive

A parent whose day is centred on childcare is not only likely to be bored, and boring to others, but is also likely to be giving an unwholesome kind of care. A baby's need is to be in the midst of an active person's life, in constant physical contact and stimulated by a great deal of the kind of experience in which he or she will take part later in life. The role of a baby while in arms is passive, with all his senses observant. He enjoys occasional direct attention, kisses, tickles, being thrown in the air, etc. But his main business is to witness the actions, interactions and surroundings of his caretaker adults or children. This information prepares babies to take their place among their people by having understood what they do. To thwart this powerful urge by looking inquiringly, so to speak, at a baby who is looking inquiringly at you, creates profound frustration; it manacles his mind. The baby's expectation of a strong, busy, central figure, to whom he can be peripheral, is undermined by an emotionally needy, servile person who is seeking his acceptance or approval. The baby will increasingly signal, but it will not be for more attention; it will actually be a demand for inclusion in adult-centred experience. Much of the frustration shown by such a baby is caused by his inability to make his signals that something is wrong bring about anything that is right.

Later on, some of the most exasperated and 'contrary' children are those whose antisocial behaviour is a plea to be shown how to behave cooperatively. Permissiveness constantly deprives children of the examples of adult-centred life where they can find the place they seek in a natural hierarchy of greater and lesser experience, and where their desirable *actions* are accepted and their undesirable *actions* rejected, while *they themselves* are always accepted. Children need to see that they are assumed to be well intentioned, naturally social people who are trying to do the right thing and want a reliable reaction from their elders to guide them. A child seeks information about what is done and not done, so if he breaks a plate he needs to see some anger or sadness at its destruction but not a withdrawal of esteem for him – as though he were not also angry or sad at having let it slip and resolving on his own initiative to be more careful.

If parents do not distinguish between desirable and undesirable acts, the child often behaves more interruptively and disruptively in order to force them to play their correct part. Then, when they cannot bear any more imposition upon their 'patience', the parents may vent all their pent-up anger on the child himself, perhaps saying they have had 'enough' of him, and send him out of sight. The implication is that all the previous behaviour they were tolerating was, in fact, bad but that they were misrepresenting their true feelings at the time and that the irremediable badness of the child finally brought their pretence of acceptance of him to an end. The game is defined this way to the children of many a household, who come to see that they are expected to try to 'get away with' as much undesirable behaviour as possible before the axe falls, when they are revealed in their true colours as unacceptable.

In extreme cases, when parents, often having had their first child late in life, dote so disastrously upon their little darlings that they never show *any* sign of distinguishing between what is to be done and what not done, the children are nearly mad with frustration. They rebel at every new 'Would you like to have this?', 'Would you like to do that?', 'What would you like to eat ... to do ... to wear?', 'What do you want Mummy to do?', etc.

I knew a most beautiful two-and-a-half-year-old girl who was treated like that. Already she never smiled. Her parents' every fawning suggestion of something that might please her was greeted with scowls of discontentment and obstinate repetitions of 'No!' Her rejection made them even more abject, and the desperate game went on, with the little girl never able to get her parents to set an example from which she could learn, as they were always looking to her for guidance. They would have given her anything she wanted but could not understand her real need to be with them as they lived their own lives as adults.

Children expend an enormous amount of energy in trying to get attention not because they need attention itself. They are signalling that their experience is unacceptable and are trying to get a care-taker's attention only in order to correct that experience. A lifelong impulse to seek attention is simply a continuation of the frustrated child's failure to get it in the first place, until the search for the initial notice becomes a goal in itself, a sort of compulsive contest of wills. So a form of parental attention that prompts more urgent signals from the child is bound to be an inappropriate one. Natural logic forbids belief in the evolution of a species with the characteristic of driving its parents to distraction by the millions. A look at the other millions in such places as Third World countries who have not had the 'privilege' of being taught to stop understanding and trusting their children reveals families living in peace and with an eager and useful addition to the family labour force in every child over the age of about four.

New Thoughts on Psychotherapy

My approach to healing the effects of the deprivations of childhood has evolved from an attempt to reproduce the missed experiences themselves to an attempt to convert the messages, conscious and unconscious, left in the psyche as a result of them. I have found, in my own practice as a psychotherapist, that one can successfully commute low or negative expectations of oneself and the world by thoroughly understanding what those expectations are, how they got there and why they are false. The most ingrained feeling of inadequacy, at its very origin, was a knowledge of one's true worthiness. This knowledge is betrayed and eroded by experiences that impose erroneous beliefs, beliefs that in infancy and childhood one is unable to question. Fears, nameless, shapeless threats of consequences too dire to contemplate, cut off any freedom of action or even thought that lies in their direction. These fears are sometimes so restricting that one is at liberty only to live one's life in the self-imposed equivalent of a prison yard.

Tracking down one of these terrors to its beginning reveals it to be an experience that, when finally envisaged by the adult, is recognized as frightening only to a child. The ceaseless, draining effort to keep oneself from coming face-to-face with that dread is automatically abandoned, and the part, large or small, of one's life that was held in thrall by it comes, at last, into its own. One can then allow oneself to do or be whatever it forbade – to be successful or to fail, to be a 'nice guy' or stop being such a nice guy, to love or to accept being loved, take risks or stop taking risks – without an inappropriate compulsion preventing the best use of one's judgement, instinctive and intellectual.

In the late 1970s, during the last of his thirty years of pioneering research in abreaction therapy, I was able to join Dr Frank Lake in some of the work at his centre in Nottingham. He had read this book and was keen to show me that the offences to people's sensibilities about which I am so concerned begin not at birth but during the equally formative time *in utero*. The dramatic reliving of these experiences by his many subjects, and subsequently some of mine, convinced me that he was right, especially since he produced the abreactions in me before I had seen anyone else curled up in foetal helplessness, moving limbs in that special way and making sounds and expressing emotions that I came to recognize as being of that time.

I still make use of this technique when a client arrives at a point where he needs to know about his birth or his early infant or intra-uterine experience, but, dramatic though it is, it has been my impression that abreacting is not often therapeutic in itself. The value of the experience lies in its contribution to the subject's information, which is then integrated into his new understanding of how things really are in his life (as opposed to how he has always believed them to be). Occasionally, an abreaction may turn up the last piece of a puzzle, making possible the leap from understanding to realization, when one's spontaneous behaviour finally comes to reflect the discovered truth. But it is the truth itself that brings about the transformation ... and only the truth, it appears, no matter how it is acquired: by determined detective work employing induction and sometimes deduction, by re-evaluating beliefs unexamined since they were formed in childhood (usually concerned with 'goodness' and 'badness') as well as through abreaction or data gleaned from others who had no investment in forgetting some event that, in its time, seemed cataclysmic to the subject. The liberating results of this process usually begin to appear quite quickly, and major transformations take months rather than years.

In the light of the continuum concept, a troubled person is an inherently 'right' creature whose species-specific needs have not been met and whose precisely evolved expectations have been greeted and treated with self-righteous denial or condemnation by those whose role should have been to respect and fulfil them. Unresponsive parents have the unfortunate effect of making a child feel that *he* has not been lovable, or deserving, or somehow 'good' enough. He cannot, by his nature, conceive them to be wrong: it must be he himself who is at fault. So when he can thoroughly realize that his crying, sulking, self-doubt, apathy or rebellion were correct human responses to his incorrect treatment, his whole feeling about himself as in the wrong changes appropriately. A review of a person's history in that light, I believe, has in itself a salutary effect and creates a healing atmosphere for someone accustomed to being made to feel unworthy, unwelcome or guilty. I have been glad to hear that many other psychotherapists have found the continuum concept useful too, for themselves, their students and the people they are treating.

Indeed, in the decade since this book first appeared a far more hospitable climate for its ideas has developed in many quarters, such as obstetrics, child care, social institutions and psychology, and in a widening search for trustworthy principles by which to live. I was particularly encouraged to see the description of a film character in a recent *Time* magazine review, which read: 'Her sense of social responsibility is informed by unimpeachable instinct, not by suspect ideology.' I hope this new edition, as well as those in other languages, will be instrumental in allowing unimpeachable instinct increasingly to inform our very suspect ideology.

London, 1985

1 : How My Ideas Were so Radically Changed

This book is meant to propound an idea, not tell a story, but I think there is a purpose to be served in telling a little of my history, something of the preparation of the ground in which the concept took root. It may help explain how my views departed so far from those of the twentieth-century Americans among whom I grew up.

I went to the South American jungles with no theory to prove, no more than normal curiosity about the Indians and only a vague sense that I might learn something of significance. In Florence, on my first trip to Europe, I was invited to join two Italian explorers on a diamond-hunting expedition in the region of Venezuela's Caroni River, a tributary of the Orinoco. It was a last-minute invitation, and I had twenty minutes to decide, race to my hotel, pack, dash to the station and jump on the train as it was pulling away from the platform.

It was very dramatic but rather frightening when the action suddenly subsided and I saw our dimly lit compartment piled with suitcases, reflected in the dusty window, and realized I was on my way to a genuine jungle.

There had not been time to take account of my reasons for wanting to go, but my response had been instant and sure. It was not the idea of the diamonds that I found irresistible, though digging one's fortune out of tropical riverbeds sounded far more attractive than any other work I could think of. It was the word *jungle* that held all the magic, perhaps because of something that happened when I was a child.

It was when I was eight and it seemed to have great importance. I still think of it as an experience of value, but like most such moments of enlightenment, it gave a glimpse of the existence of an order without revealing its construction or how one could sustain a view of it in the muddle of day-to-day living. Most disappointing of all, the conviction that I had seen the elusive truth at last did little or nothing towards guiding my footsteps through the muddle. The brief vision was too fragile to survive the trip back to applicability. Although it had to contend with all my mundane motivations and, most disastrously, with the power of habit, perhaps it is worth mentioning, for it was a hint of that sense of rightness (for want of a less clumsy phrase) the search for which this book is about.

The incident happened during a nature walk in the Maine woods where I was at summer camp. I was last in the queue; I had fallen back a bit and was hurrying to catch up when, through the trees, I saw a glade. It had a lush fir tree at the far side and a knoll in the centre covered in bright, almost luminous, green moss. The rays of the afternoon sun slanted against the blue-black green of the pine forest. The little roof of visible sky was perfectly blue. The whole picture had a completeness, an all-there quality, of such dense power that it stopped me in my tracks. I went to the edge and then, softly, as though into a magical or holy place, to the centre, where I sat, then lay down with my cheek against the freshness of the moss. It is here, I thought, and I felt the anxiety that coloured my life fall away. This, at last, was where things were as they ought to be. Everything was in its place – the tree, the earth underneath, the rock, the moss. In autumn it would be right; in winter, under the snow, it would be perfect in its wintriness. Spring would come again and miracle within miracle would unfold, each at its special pace, some things having died off, some sprouting in their first spring, but all of equal and utter rightness.

I felt I had discovered the missing centre of things, the key to rightness itself, and must hold on to this knowledge that was so clear in that place. I was tempted for a moment to take a scrap of moss away with me, to keep as a reminder; but a rather grown-up thought prevented me. I suddenly feared that in treasuring an amulet of moss, I might lose the real prize: the insight I had had – that I might think my vision safe as long as I kept the moss, only to find one day that I had nothing but a pinch of dead vegetation.

So I took nothing but promised myself I would remember The Glade every night before going to sleep and in that way never be far from its stabilizing power. I knew, even at eight, that the confusion of values thrust upon me by parents, teachers, other children, nannies, camp counsellors and others would only worsen as I grew up. The years would add complications and steer me into more and more impenetrable tangles of rights and wrongs, desirables and undesirables. I had already seen enough to know that. But if I could keep The Glade with me, I thought, I would never be lost.

That night in my camp bed I brought The Glade to mind, was filled with gratitude and renewed my vow to preserve my vision. And for years its quality was undiminished as I saw the knoll, the fir, the light, the wholeness in my mind every night.

But as more years went by, I often found that I had forgotten The Glade for days, or weeks, at a time. I tried to recapture the sense of salvation that had formerly infused it. But my world widened. The simpler sort of good-girl-bad-girl values of the nursery had gradually been overrun by the often conflicting values of my sector of the culture and of my family, a mixture of Victorian virtues and graces with a strong bent towards individualism, liberal views and artistic talents and, above all, high regard for a brilliant and original intellect like my mother's.

By the time I was about fifteen, I realized with a hollow sadness (since I could not remember what I was mourning) that I had lost the meaning of The Glade. I recalled perfectly the woodland scene, but, as I had feared when I abstained from taking the souvenir bit of moss, its significance had escaped. Instead, my mental picture of The Glade had become the empty amulet.

I lived with my grandmother, and when she died I decided to go to Europe, though I had not finished university. My thoughts were not very clear during my grief, but because turning to my mother always ended in my being hurt, I felt I had to make a giant effort to get on my own feet. Nothing I was expected to want seemed worth having – jobs writing for fashion magazines, a career as a model or further education.

In my cabin on the ship bound for France, I wept for fear I had gambled away everything familiar to me for a hope of something nameless. But I did not want to turn back.

I wandered about Paris sketching and writing poetry. I was offered a job as a model at Dior but did not take it. I had connections on

French *Vogue* but did not use them except for occasional modelling jobs that entailed no commitment. But I felt more at home in that foreign country than I ever had in my native New York. I felt that I was on the right track, but I still could not have said what I was looking for. In the summer I went to Italy, first to Venice and then, after a visit to a villa in the Lombard countryside, to Florence. There I met the two young Italians who invited me to Venezuela to hunt for diamonds. Again, as on my departure from America, I was frightened by the boldness of the step I was taking but never for an instant considered retreat.

When at last the expedition began, after many preparations and delays, we travelled up the Carcupi River, a small unexplored tributary of the Caroni. In a month we made considerable headway upriver in spite of the obstacles, mainly trees fallen across the water, through which we had to cut a passage for the canoe with axes and machetes, or waterfalls or rapids over which we portaged about a ton of *matériel* with the help of two Indians. The little river had halved in volume by the time we made a base camp to explore some tributary streamlets.

It was our first day of rest since we had entered the Carcupi. After breakfast the Italian leader and both Indians went off to look at the geological situation, while the second Italian lolled gratefully in his hammock.

I took one of the two paperback books I had bought from a small selection of English titles at the Ciudad Bolivar airport and found a seat among the roots of a large tree that overhung the river. I read partway through the first chapter, not day-dreaming but following the story with normal attentiveness, when suddenly I was struck with terrific force by a realization. 'This is it! The Glade!' All the excitement of the little girl's insight came back. I had lost it, and now in a grown-up Glade, the biggest jungle on earth, it had returned. The mysteries of jungle life, the ways of its animals and plants, its dramatic storms and sunsets, its snakes, its orchids, its fascinating virginity, the hardness of making one's way in it and the generosity of its beauty all made it appear even more actively and profoundly right. It was rightness on a grand scale. As we flew over, it had looked like a great green ocean, stretching to the horizon on every side, interlaced with waterways, raised high upon assertive mountains, offered to the sky on the open hands of plateaux. It vibrated in its every cell with life, with rightness – ever-changing, ever-intact and always perfect.

In my joy that day I thought that I had come to the end of my search, that my goal had been achieved: the clear view of things at their undiluted best. It was the 'rightness' I had tried to discern through the bafflements of my childhood and – in the talks, discussions, arguments, often pursued until dawn, in the hope of a glimpse of it – in my adolescent years. It was The Glade, lost, found and now recognized, this time for ever. Around me, overhead, underfoot, everything was right, being born, living, dying and being replaced without a break in the order of it all.

I ran my hands lovingly over the great roots that held me like an armchair and began to entertain the idea of staying in the jungle for the rest of my life.

At the end of the Carcupi exploration (we did find a few diamonds), when we went back to the little outpost of Los Caribes for supplies, I saw in a mirror that I had gained weight and for the first time in my life might be described as slender rather than skinny. I felt stronger, more able, less afraid than ever before. I was thriving in my beloved jungle. There were still six months to think about how I'd manage to stay on after the expedition; there was no need to face the practical problems yet.

When the months had passed, however, I was ready to leave. My flourishing health had been brought down by malaria, and my morale was eroded by hunger for meat and green vegetables. I would have traded one of our hard-won diamonds for a glass of orange juice. And I was thinner than ever.

But after seven and a half months I had a far more detailed view of the jungle's rightness. I had seen the Tauripan Indians, not just the two we had hired but whole clans, families at home in their huts, travelling in groups, hunting, living the life of a species in its habitat, without outside support of any consequence except for the machete and the steel axe in place of their original stone one. They were the happiest people I had seen anywhere, but I hardly noticed it then; they were so different from us, smaller, less muscular, yet able to carry heavier loads much greater distances than the best of us. I did not so much as wonder why. They thought in other patterns. ('To get to Padacapah,' one of us would ask, 'shall we go upriver by canoe, or march overland?' and an Indian would answer, 'Yes.') I seldom had a clear sense that they were of the same species as ourselves, though, of course, if asked, I should have *said* so without hesitation. The children were uniformly well behaved: they never fought, were never punished, always obeyed happily and instantly. The deprecation 'Boys will be boys' did not apply to them, but I never asked myself why. There was no doubt in my mind that the jungle was right, nor that whatever I was looking for was best looked for there, but the rightness and viability of the jungle's ecosystem, plants, animals, Indians and all, did not, as I first believed, automatically constitute an answer, a personal solution, for me.

Again, this was not then clear. I was slightly ashamed of my increasing desire for spinach, orange juice, rest. I had a wildly romantic love for, and awe of, the great, uncaring forest and, while preparing to leave, was already thinking of ways and means to come back. The truth of the matter was that I had found no rightness for myself at all. I had only seen it from outside and managed to recognize it, and very superficially at that. I somehow did not see the obvious: that the Indians, as humans like myself and also as participants in the jungle's rightness, were the common denominator, the link between the harmony around me and my want of it.

Some small illuminations did get through to my civilization-blinded mind: for example, some concerning the concept of work. We had traded our slightly too small aluminium canoe for a much too big dugout. In this vessel carved from a single tree, seventeen Indians at one time travelled with us. With all their baggage added to ours and everyone aboard, the vast canoe still looked rather empty. Portaging it, this time with only four or five Indians to help, over half a mile of boulders beside a large waterfall was depressing to contemplate. It meant placing logs across the path of the canoe and hauling it, inch by inch, in the merciless sun, slipping inevitably into the crevices between the boulders whenever the canoe pivoted out of control and scraping one's shins, ankles and whatever else one landed on against the granite. We had done the portage before with the small canoe, and the two Italians and I, knowing what lay ahead, spent several days dreading the hard work and pain. On the day we arrived at Arepuchi Falls we were primed to suffer and started off, grim-faced and hating every moment, to drag the thing over the rocks.

When it swung sideways, so heavy was the rogue pirogue, it several times pinned one of us to the burning rock until the others could move it off. A quarter of the way across all ankles were bleeding. Partly by way of begging off for a minute, I jumped up on a high rock to photograph the scene. From my vantage point and momentary disinvolvement, I noticed a most interesting fact. Here before me were several men engaged in a single task. Two, the Italians, were tense, frowning, losing their tempers at everything and swearing non-stop in the distinctive manner of the Tuscan. The rest, Indians, were having a fine time. They were laughing at the unwieldiness of the canoe, making a game of the battle; they relaxed between pushes, laughing at their own scrapes and were especially amused when the canoe, as it wobbled forward, pinned one, then another, underneath it. The fellow held bare-backed against the scorching granite, when he could breathe again, invariably laughed the loudest, enjoying his relief.

All were doing the same work; all were experiencing strain and pain. There was no difference in our situations except that *we* had been conditioned by our culture to believe that such a combination of circumstances constituted an unquestionable low on the scale of well-being and were quite unaware that we had any option in the matter.

The Indians, on the other hand, equally unconscious of making a choice, were in a particularly merry state of mind, revelling in the camaraderie; and, of course, they had had no long build-up of dread to mar the preceding days. Each forward move was for them a little victory. As I finished photographing and rejoined the team, I opted out of the civilized choice and enjoyed, quite genuinely, the rest of the portage. Even the barks and bruises I sustained were reduced with remarkable ease to nothing more significant than what they indeed were: small hurts which would soon heal and which required neither an unpleasant emotional reaction, such as anger, self-pity or resentment, nor anxiety at how many more there might be before the end of the haul. On the contrary, I found myself appreciative of my excellently designed body, which would patch itself up with no instructions or decisions from me.

But soon my sense of emancipation again gave way to the tyranny of habit, to the great weight of cultural conditioning that only a sustained conscious effort can countermand. I did not make the necessary effort and therefore came away from the expedition without much profit from the revelation.

Another hint about human nature and work came later.

Two Indian families lived in a hut overlooking a magnificent white beach, a lagoon in a wide crescent of rocks, the Caroni and Arepuchi Falls beyond. One paterfamilias was called Pepe, the other Cesar. It was Pepe who told the story.

It seems that Cesar had been 'adopted' by Venezuelans when very young and had gone to live with them in a small town. He was sent to school, learned to read and write and was reared as a Venezuelan. When he was grown, he came, like many of the men of those Guianese towns, to the upper Caroni to try his luck at diamond hunting. He was working with a group of Venezuelans when he was recognized by Mundo, chief of the Tauripans at Guayparu.

'Were you not taken to live with José Grande?' Mundo asked.

'I was brought up by José Grande,' said Cesar, according to the story.

'Then you have come back to your own people. You are a Tauripan,' said Mundo.

Whereupon Cesar, after a great deal of thought, decided that he would be better off living as an Indian than as a Venezuelan and came to Arepuchi where Pepe lived.

For five years Cesar lived with Pepe's family, marrying a pretty Tauripan woman and becoming the father of a little girl. As Cesar did not like to work, he and his wife and daughter ate the food grown on Pepe's plantation. Cesar was delighted to find that Pepe did not expect him to clear a garden of his own or even help with the work in his. Pepe enjoyed working and since Cesar did not, the arrangement suited everyone.

Cesar's wife liked joining the other women and girls in cutting and preparing the cassava to eat, but all Cesar liked was hunting tapir and, occasionally, other game. After a couple of years he developed a taste for fishing and added his catches to those of Pepe and his two sons, who always liked to fish and who had supplied his family as generously as theirs.

Just before we arrived, Cesar decided to clear a garden of his own, and Pepe helped with every detail, from choosing the site to felling and burning the trees. Pepe enjoyed it all the more because he and his friend talked and joked the whole time.

Cesar, after five years' assurance, felt that no one was pushing him into the project and was as free to enjoy working as Pepe or any other Indian.

Everyone at Arepuchi was glad, Pepe told us, because Cesar had been growing discontented and irritable. 'He wanted to make a garden of his own,' Pepe laughed, 'but he didn't know it himself!' Pepe thought it hilarious that anyone should not know that he wanted to work.

For me, these odd clues that we in civilization were labouring under some rather serious misapprehensions about man's nature did not, at the time, suggest any general principles on the subject. But even if I did not form an idea of what I wanted to know, or even a clear notion that I was engaged in a search, at least I recognized that I had found a path worth following. It was enough to keep me on course for the next few years.

The second expedition, to a region six weeks from the utmost marches of Spanish-speaking Venezuela, was led by another Italian, a professor who felt strongly that girls had no business in jungles. One of my former partners managed to get me a grudging acceptance none the less, and I was able to follow my path to the Stone Age world of the Yequana and Sanema tribes, preserved from outside by what was called 'impenetrable' rain forest, in the upper Caura River basin near the Brazilian border.

The strongly individual personalities of the men, women and children were even more evident here because there had never been any need to cultivate a defensive blank-face-for-strangers like the Tauripans', but in that utterly foreign land I failed to notice that much of the unreal quality of its people was accounted for by an absence of unhappiness, a large factor in every society familiar to me. I must have had a vague notion that somewhere behind the trees, just out of sight, the ghost of Cecil B. De Mille was directing the proceedings in classic, one-dimensional, Hollywood-savage style. The 'rules' of human behaviour did not apply to them.

For three weeks, during which my partners said that they had been unavoidably detained by a large band of pygmies who kept them as pets, I lived alone with the Yequana. In that short time I unlearned more of the assumptions upon which I was reared than I had on the entire first expedition. And I began to see the value of the unlearning process. Several more contributions to an alternative point of view on the subject of work, too, penetrated past the intervening layers of my prejudice.

One was the apparent absence of a word for 'work' in the Yequana vocabulary. They had the word *tarabaho* to use about dealings with non-Indians, who, apart from us, were known to them almost entirely by hearsay. This was a slight mispronunciation of the Spanish *trabajo* and referred quite accurately to what the *conquistadores* and their successors meant by it. It struck me that it was the only Spanish derivative among all the words I learned from them. There appeared to be no Yequana concept of work similar to ours. There were words for each activity that might have been included but no generic term.

If they did not distinguish work from other ways of spending time, it was little wonder that they behaved so irrationally (as I then judged) about fetching water. The women left their firesides several times a day, carrying two or three small gourds at a time, walked part of the way down the mountain, picked their way down a precipitous slope that was extremely slippery when wet, filled the gourds from a streamlet and climbed back to the village above. The whole operation took about twenty minutes. Many of them carried babies as well as gourds.

When I went down for the first time, I was struck by the inconvenience of walking so far for a commodity so constantly needed. It was inconceivable that they should not choose a village site where water was more accessible. The last part of the walk, at the stream bank, made me tense with anxiety at the necessity for taking care at every step to avoid falling. To be sure, the Yequana have a superior sense of balance and, like the North American Indian, no fear of heights, but the fact was that neither they nor I ever fell, and I alone resented having to pay attention to my steps. Their steps were equally cautious, but they did not frown as I did at the 'hardship' of taking care. They went on gossiping and joking softly, on the flat or on the slope, for they usually went in groups of two, three or more, and, as always, a party mood prevailed.

Once a day each woman put her gourds and clothing (a small, apronlike *cache-sexe*, and ankle, knee, wrist, upper arm, neck and ear beads) on the bank and bathed herself and her baby. However many women and children participated, the bath had a Roman quality of luxuriousness. Every move bespoke sensual enjoyment, and the babies were handled like objects so marvellous that their owners felt constrained to put a mock-modest face on their pleasure and pride. Walking down the mountain was done in the same accustomed-to-the-best, almost smug, style and their last perilous steps into the stream would have done credit to a Miss World coming forward to claim her crown. This was true of all the Yequana women and girls I saw, though their distinct personalities rendered the manifestations of their cosiness quite various.

Upon reflection, I was hard put to think of a 'better' way to use the water-fetching time, at least from the point of view of well-being. If, on the other hand, progress – or its handmaidens, speed, efficiency and novelty – were the criterion, the water walks were positively moronic. But my experience of the ingenuity of the people in question was such that I had no doubt that, had I asked them to invent a means of precluding my going to the stream for water, they would have put together some bamboo pipes or a pulley to help me deal with the slippery bit, or built me a hut near the stream. They themselves had no motive to progress, as they felt no need, no pressure from any quarter, to change their ways.

That I deemed it an imposition to have to make use of my perfectly adequate coordination, or resented, from unexamined principle, the use of time to fill a need, was an arbitrary assignment of values that their culture did not share.

Another insight about work came more as an experience than an observation. Anchu, chief of the Yequana village, made a practice of guiding me, whenever he had the chance, towards happier behaviour. I had just traded a glass ornament for seven canes of sugar, and I was in the process also of assimilating a lesson, which I shall mention later, about trading technique among people whose good relations are more important than their bargains. Anchu's wife started back to their hut in an isolated place nearby, and Anchu, a Sanema who seemed to be his butler, and I were to return over two mountains to the village atop a third. The seven stalks were on the ground where the wife had left them. Anchu directed the Sanema brave to take three, and himself took another three on his shoulder, leaving one on the ground. I expected the men to carry it all, and when Anchu pointed to the last cane and said, 'Amaadeh' ('You'), I was for an instant annoyed at the idea that I was ordered to carry something on the steep path back when there were two strong men to do it; but just in time I was reminded that Anchu sooner or later turned out to know best about almost anything.

I shouldered the cane, and as Anchu waited for me to lead the way I started the first ascent. The burden of dread of the long walk back, accumulated on the way down and hardened through lunch at Anchu's and time at the cane garden, was now compounded by the news that I was to have a heavy cane to carry as well. The first few steps were weighted with the thought of the strain I always experienced on treks through jungles, especially uphill and when carrying anything that did not leave my hands free.

But quite suddenly all that added weight fell away. Anchu gave not the slightest sign that I ought to walk faster, that my prestige would suffer if I kept a comfortable pace, that I was being judged for my performance or that time on the path was in any way less desirable than time after arrival.

Hurry had always been a factor in similar exercises with my white partners, as had anxiety about keeping up with the men, preserving the honour of the fair sex and the uncontested assumption that the occasion was unpleasant because it tested one's physical endurance and moral determination. This time the very different demeanour of Anchu and the Sanema removed these elements and left me simply walking in the jungle with a sugar cane on my shoulder. Gone was any sense of competition, and the physical strain turned from an imposition upon my body to a satisfying proof of its strength, while my teeth-gritting will power in the face of martyrdom no longer applied.

Then a new pleasure added itself to my freedom: I was aware of carrying not just a stick of cane but part of a load shared among three companions. I had heard about 'team spirit' until it ceased to connote anything but pretence at school and summer camp. One's own position had always been at risk. One always felt threatened, watched, judged. The straightforward business of doing a task in partnership with a fellow being was lost in a tangle of competitiveness; the primordial feeling of pleasure at pooling one's forces with those of others had never had a chance to arise.

On the way, I was astonished at the speed and ease with which I was walking. Usually, drenched with perspiration and pushing my limits, I would have been moving no more quickly. Perhaps I was catching a glimpse of the Indians' secret of outdoing our well nourished strongmen despite their generally inferior muscle power. They were economizing their forces by using them only to do the job, wasting none on associated tensions.

I was reminded of my surprise at the Tauripans on the first expedition when, loaded down with about seventy-five pounds each on their backs and carefully crossing a 'bridge' consisting of a single narrow log felled across a stream, one of them would think of a joke and stop in mid-log, turn around, tell the story to the men piling up behind him and then proceed across while he and his friends all laughed in their peculiarly musical way. It never occurred to me that they were not suffering as we did under the circumstances, so their merriment gave a strange, almost lunatic impression. (It was in fact very like their habit of telling a joke in the middle of the night, when everyone was asleep. Though some were snoring loudly, all would awaken instantly, laugh and in seconds resume sleep, snoring and all. They did not feel that being awake was more unpleasant than being asleep, and they awoke fully alert, as when a distant pack of dangerous peccary was heard by all the Indians simultaneously, though they had been asleep, while I, awake and listening to the sounds of the surrounding jungle, had noticed nothing.) Like most travellers, I had watched their unfamiliar behaviour without comprehending it and never attempted to bridge the gap between their expression of human nature and ours.

But on that second expedition I acquired a taste for the new ideas that came of opening closed subjects, such as 'Progress is good', 'Man must make laws to live by', 'A child belongs to its parents', 'Leisure is pleasanter than work'.

Expeditions Three and Four, under my own leadership, one four and the other nine months long, took me back to the same region, and the process continued. My journals reflect that the unlearning technique was becoming second nature to me, but the broader unquestioned premises upon which my own culture founded its view of the human condition, such as the one that unhappiness is as legitimate a part of experience as happiness and necessary in order to render happiness appreciable, or that it is more advantageous to be young than to be old: those still took me a long time to pry loose for re-examination.

At the end of the fourth trip I returned to New York with my head full of all that I had seen and a point of view so stripped of presuppositions that the effect was like arriving, after a long haul, at zero. I held my observations like separate pieces of a jigsaw puzzle, reluctant to put anything together, accustomed by now to dissecting anything that looked suspiciously like a group of behaviour patterns posing as a principle of human nature.

It was not until an editor asked me to write a piece elaborating a statement of mine quoted in the *New York Times** that I began to reverse the tearing-down process and, bit by bit, to perceive the order that underlay not only my South American observations but also the naked fragments into which I had broken my experience of civilized life.

Still, at that juncture I was innocent of theory; but, as I looked about with unblinkered eyes, I saw for the first time some of the distortions in the personalities around me and began to understand some of the distorting forces as well. After about a year I also recognized the evolutionary origins of human expectations and tendencies that began to explain the high state of well-being of my savage friends compared with the civilized.

Before discussing these ideas in a book I thought it best to make a fifth expedition. I wanted to look again at the Yequana, this time with my newly formed views in mind, to see whether my observations, rallied only retrospectively into a body of evidence, might be usefully augmented by deliberate study.

* 'I would be ashamed to admit to the Indians that where I come from the women do not feel themselves capable of raising children until they read the instructions written by a strange man.'

The airstrip we cleared on the second expedition, and used on the third and fourth, had become the site of a mission house and a weather station, both abandoned. The Yequana, despite the acquisition of shirts and trousers by some of their number, were reassuringly unchanged, and the neighbouring Sanema, though reduced by disease to near-extinction, held equally firm to their ancient and proven manner of life.

Both tribes were willing to work or barter for gifts from outside but not to trade any part of their views, traditions or way of life for them. Several shotguns and some torches created in their possessors a moderate desire for powder, shot, percussion caps and batteries, but not enough to make them do any work they did not enjoy, nor pursue a task after it had become tedious.

Some details that had escaped casual observation, such as whether or not children are present during the sexual act of their parents, were filled in by questioning, as well as others, like their view of the universe, mythology, shamanic doings, et cetera, which had relevance to the sort of culture it is that suits human nature so well.

But in the main, Expedition Five served to assure me that my interpretation of their behaviour, constructed from my recollections of it, was supported by the reality. Indeed, the once unaccountable actions of Indians of both tribes, viewed in the light of continuum principles, became not only understandable but often predictable.

In my search for exceptions that might point out flaws in my reasoning, I found that they consistently 'proved the rule', as in the case of a baby who sucked his thumb, stiffened his body and screamed like a civilized baby but who presented no mystery, as he had been taken away shortly after birth by the missionary and kept in a Caracas hospital for eight months until his illness was cured and he could be returned to his family.

Dr Robert Coles, the child psychiatrist and writer, called in by an American foundation to appraise my ideas, told me he had been invited as 'an expert in the field' but that 'the field, unfortunately, does not yet exist' and neither he nor anyone else could be considered an authority in it. The continuum concept must therefore be evaluated on its own merits, as it touches, or not, those half-buried senses and faculties in each person that it sets out to describe and reinstate.

For some two million years, despite being the same species of animal as ourselves, man was a success. He had evolved from apehood to manhood as a hunter-gatherer with an efficient lifestyle which, had it continued, might have seen him through many a million-year anniversary. As it is, most ecologists agree, his chances of surviving even another century are diminished with each day's activities.

During the brief few thousand years since he strayed from the way of life to which evolution adapted him, he has not only wreaked havoc upon the natural order of the entire planet, but he has also managed to bring into disrepute the highly evolved good sense that guided his behaviour throughout all those aeons. Much of it has been undermined only recently as the last coverts of our instinctive competence are rooted out and subjected to the uncomprehending gaze of science. Ever more frequently our innate sense of what is best for us is short-circuited by suspicion while the intellect, which has never known much about our real needs, decides what to do.

It is not, for example, the province of the reasoning faculty to decide how a baby ought to be treated. We have had exquisitely precise instincts, expert in every detail of child care, since long before we became anything resembling *Homo sapiens*. But we have conspired to baffle this longstanding knowledge so utterly that we now employ researchers full time to puzzle out how we should behave towards children, one another and ourselves. It is no secret that the experts have not 'discovered' how to live satisfactorily, but the more they fail, the more they attempt to bring the problems under the sole influence of reason and disallow what reason cannot understand or control.

We are now fairly brought to heel by the intellect; our inherent sense of what is good for us has been undermined to the point where we are barely aware of its working and cannot tell an original impulse from a distorted one.

But I believe it is still possible to start as we are, lost and handicapped, and find a way back. At least we might learn the direction in which our best interests lie and not go on making efforts that have an equal chance of leading us further off the track. The conscious part of the mind, like a good 'technical adviser' in someone else's war, when it sees the error of its ways, ought to work to put itself out of business, not move deeper into alien territory. There are, of course, plenty of jobs for our ability to reason without its usurping the work which has for many million years been managed by the infinitely more refined and knowledgeable areas of the mind called instinct. If they too were conscious, they would deluge our heads out of commission in an instant, if for no other reason than that the conscious mind, by its nature, can consider only one thing at a time, while the unconscious can make any number of observations, calculations, syntheses and executions simultaneously and correctly.

'Correct' in this context is a tricky word. It does not imply that we all agree on what we want the results of our actions to be, as our intellectual ideas of what we want vary from person to person. *What is meant here by 'correct' is that which is appropriate to the ancient continuum of our species inasmuch as it is suited to the tendencies and expectations with which we evolved.* Expectation, in this sense, is founded as deeply in man as his very design. His lungs not only have, but can be said to *be*, an expectation of air; his eyes are an expectation of light rays of the specific range of wavelengths sent out by what is useful for him to see at the hours appropriate for his species to see them; his ears are an expectation of vibrations caused by the events most likely to concern him, including the voices of other people; and his own voice is an expectation of ears functioning similarly in them. The list can be extended indefinitely: waterproof skin and hair – expectation of rain; hairs in nose – expectation of dust; pigmentation in skin – expectation of sun; perspiratory mechanism – expectation of heat; coagulatory mechanism – expectation of accidents to body surfaces; one sex – expectation of the other; reflex mechanism – expectation of the need for speed of reaction in emergencies.

How do the forces that put him together know in advance what a human will need? The secret is experience. The chain of experience that prepares a human being for his time on earth begins with the adventures of the first single-celled unit of living matter. What it experienced in the way of temperature, the composition of its surroundings, available nourishment to fuel its activities, weather changes and bumpings into other objects or members of its own species was passed on to its descendants. Upon these data, transmitted by means still largely mysterious to science, the very, very slow changes came about which, after an unimaginable passage of time, produced a variety of forms that could survive and reproduce themselves by coping with the environment in different ways.

As always happens when a system diversifies and becomes more complex, more precisely adapted to a wider variety of circumstance, the effect was greater stability. Life itself was less in danger of extinction by natural catastrophe. Then even if one whole form of life was wiped out, there were plenty of others which would carry on and also carry on complicating, diversifying, adapting, stabilizing. (It seems a reasonably safe guess that quite a few 'first' forms were extinguished before one survived, perhaps millions of years after the last one, and diversified in time to avoid being snuffed out by some intolerable elemental event.)

At the same time, the stabilizing principle was at work in each form and each part of each form, taking its data from its inheritance of experience, from its contacts of every kind, and equipping its descendants in ever more complex ways to deal more efficiently with those experiences. *Therefore the design of each individual was a reflection of the experience it expected to encounter.* The experience it could tolerate was defined by the circumstances to which its antecedents had adapted.

If the evolving creatures had been formed in a climate that never exceeded 120°F for more than a few hours nor fell below 45°, the going form could do the same; but no more than its ancestors could it maintain its well-being if exposed to excessively long bouts at the extremes of its tolerance. The emergency reserves would be drained, and if relief were not forthcoming, death would follow, for individual or species. *If one wants to know what is correct for any species, one must know the inherent expectations of that species.*

How much do we know about the inherent expectations of man?

We know quite well what he gets, and we are often told what he wants, or *should* want, according to the current system of values. But what his evolutionary history has conditioned him to expect as the latest specimen in his ancient line of inheritance is, ironically, one of the darker mysteries. Intellect has taken over deciding what is best and insists on sovereignty for its vogues and guesses. Consequently, what was once man's confident expectation of suitable treatment and surroundings is now so frustrated that a person often thinks himself lucky if he is not actually homeless or in pain. But even as he is saying, 'I'm all right,' there is in him a sense of loss, a longing for something he cannot name, a feeling of being off-centre, of missing something. Asked point-blank, he will seldom deny it.

So, to discover the precise character of his evolved expectations, there is no point in looking at the late-model, civilized example.

To look at other species can be helpful but may also be misleading. Where the level of development corresponds, comparisons with other animals may be valid, as in the case of older, deeper and more fundamental needs that antecede our anthropoid form, like the requirement for air to breathe, which arose hundreds of millions of years ago and is shared by many of our fellow animals. But to study human subjects who have not left the continuum of appropriate behaviour and environment is obviously more useful. Even if we manage to identify some of our expectations which are less evident than air to breathe, there will always remain a great mass of more subtle expectations to define before we can even call on a computer to help us catch up with some small fraction of our instinctive knowledge of them. It is therefore essential to keep a constant watch for opportunities to reinstate our *innate* ability to choose what is suitable. The clumsy intellect with which we must now try to recognize it can then occupy itself with tasks it is better able to do.

The expectations with which we confront life are inextricably involved with tendencies (for example, to suckle, to avoid physical harm, to crawl, to explore, to imitate). As what we expect in the way of treatment and circumstance becomes available, sets of tendencies in us interact with them, again as the experience of our ancestors has prepared them to do. When the expected does not take place, corrective or compensatory tendencies make an effort to restore stability.

This human continuum can be defined as the sequence of experience that corresponds to the expectations and tendencies of our species in an environment consistent with that in which those expectations and tendencies were formed. It includes appropriate behaviour in, and treatment by, other people as part of that environment.

The continuum of an individual is whole, yet forms part of the continuum of his family, which in turn is part of his clan's, community's and species' continua, just as the continuum of the human species forms part of that of all life. Each continuum has its own expectations and tendencies, which spring from long, formative precedent. Even the continuum that includes every living thing expects, from experience of it, a suitable range of factors in the inorganic surroundings.

In each life-form the tendency to evolve is not random but furthers its own interests. It is directed at greater stability – that is, at greater diversity, complexity and therefore adaptability.

This is not at all what we call 'progress'. In fact, *resistance* to change, no way in conflict with the tendency to evolve, is an indispensable force in keeping any system stable.

What interrupted our own innate resistance to change a few thousand years ago we can only guess. The important thing is to understand the significance of evolution versus (unevolved) change. They are at diametrical cross purposes, for what evolving creates in the way of diversification, ever more precisely adapted to our requirements, change destroys by introducing behaviour or circumstances which do not take into account the entire range of factors concerned in serving our best interests. All change can do is to replace a piece of well integrated behaviour with one that is not. It replaces what is complex and adapted with what is simpler and less adapted. As a consequence, change places a strain on the equilibrium of all the intricately related factors inside and outside the system.

Evolution, then, creates stability; change brings vulnerability.

Social organizations, too, follow these rules. An evolved culture, a way of life for a group of people that fulfil their social expectations, can be any one of an infinite variety of structures. The superficial features of these structures are the most variable, their basic tenets the least, and in certain fundamental respects they are bound to be identical. They would be resistant to change, having evolved over a long period of time like any stable system in nature. It would also follow that the less the intellect interfered with instinct in the formation of behaviour patterns, the less rigid the structure would need to be on the surface (about behavioural detail, ritual, requirements for conformity) and the more inflexible at its core (in attitude towards self and towards the rights of others, sensitivity to the signals of instinct that favour survival, health, pleasure, a balance of types of activity, an impulse towards the preservation of the species, economical use of the plants and animals in the environment, and so on). In a word, the more a culture relies upon the intellect to decide policy and rules, the more restraints on the individual are necessary to maintain it.

There is no essential difference between purely instinctive behaviour, with its expectations and tendencies, and our equally instinctive expectation of a suitable culture, one in which we can develop our tendencies and fulfil our expectations, first of precise treatment in infancy and gradually of a (more flexible) *kind* of treatment and circumstance and a range of requirements to which adaptation is ready, eager and able to be made.

The role of a culture in human life is as legitimate as that of a language. Both begin with the expectation and the tendency to find their content in the environment. The social behaviour of a child develops among expected influences and examples set him by his society. Innate drives also impel him to do what he perceives is expected of him by his fellow humans; the fellow humans let him know what they do expect, according to the culture. Learning is a process of fulfilling expectations for certain kinds of information. The kinds increase in a definite order of complexity, as do the patterns of speech.

Suitability to the standards of our expectations, maintained by each individual's continuum sense (encouraged by pleasure, kept on course by a natural revulsion that mounts as the limits of appropriateness are approached), is the foundation of the viable culture's system of rights and wrongs. The particularities of the system can, again, vary infinitely so long as they remain within the essential parameters. There is plenty of room for differences, individual or tribal, without transgressing those limits.

3 : The Beginning of Life

During his time in the womb the little human being needs to be permitted to follow in a straight line from his antecedents' developmental stages, from single cell through amphibian and on to *Homo sapiens* ready for birth, without much happening to him for which his ancestors' experience in the womb has not prepared him. He is usually nourished, kept warm and jostled about pretty much as embryonic hunter-gatherers were. The sounds he hears are not very different unless his mother lives on a supersonic flight path, goes in for high-decibel discotheques or drives a lorry. He hears her heartbeat and her voice and the voices of other people and animals. He hears the sounds of her body digesting, snoring, laughing, singing, coughing and so on and is undisturbed, for his adaptations have taken them into account over the millions of years his predecessors heard similar sounds, equally loud, equally sudden. Because of their experience, he is *expecting* the sounds, the jostling and the sudden moves; they form part of the experience he requires for completion of his pre-natal development.

At birth a baby has developed far enough in his maximum-security cell to emerge and continue his life in the enormously less sheltered world outside. The shock is absorbed in part by mechanisms like high gamma globulin as protection against infection, which decreases slowly enough for him to have begun to develop immunities; limited vision, which gives way gradually to full vision well after the birthday shock is past; and a general programme of development that keys in many aspects of his make-up, such as reflexes, circulatory system and hearing before birth, and others, days, weeks or months afterwards, including the stage-by-stage coming into play of the parts of the brain.

At the moment of birth itself there is the radical change of the immediate surroundings from wet to dry, the change to a lower temperature, the suddenly unmuffled sounds, the switch-over to the baby's own ability to breathe for his oxygen supply and a change of position from head down to head level with, or above, the rest of the body. But the baby can sustain these and all the other new sensations of natural birth with amazing equanimity.

His own voice does not surprise him, though it is inside his head, very loud and never before heard, because it *has* been heard by the informants of his flesh, the makers of his ability to fear and to distinguish the fearful from the normal. When his forebears developed a voice, they also developed a network of stabilizing capabilities to smooth its advent into the continuum of what was then their species. As the voice evolved with the whole evolving of the species from one form to another and took on variations to suit the ever more complex organism, more devices developed to keep it in balance with the self and the society in which it was to be used. Ears were tuned to it; reflexes were tuned to it and infant expectations included the sound of it among the 'surprises' of the first experiences outside the womb.

In the earliest stages after birth an infant is in a state of consciousness that is all sensation; he has no capacity for thought, in the sense of reason, conscious memory, reflection or judgement. Perhaps he cannot be said to be conscious so much as sentient. Asleep, he is aware of his state of well-being, somewhat as an adult who shares a bed with a mate sleeps aware of the presence or absence of the partner. Awake, he is far more aware of his condition but in a manner that in an adult would still be called subliminal. In either state he is more vulnerable to his experience than an adult, for he has no precedent with which to qualify his impressions.

The lack of a sense of the passage of time is no disadvantage to an infant in the womb or in arms – he simply feels right; but to an infant not in arms the inability to mitigate any part of his suffering by means of hope (which depends on a sense of time) is perhaps the cruellest aspect of his ordeal. His crying, therefore, cannot even contain hope, though it acts as a signal to bring relief. Later, as the weeks and months pass and the infant's awareness increases, hope is dimly felt and crying becomes an act connected with a result, either negative or positive. But the long hours of waiting are little improved by the dawning of a sense of time. Lack of previous experience leaves time seeming intolerably long for a baby in a state of want.

Even years later, at the age of five, the promise of a bicycle 'next Christmas' is, in August, approximately as satisfying as no promise at all. At ten, time has pulled itself together in the light of experience to the extent that the child can wait a day more or less comfortably for some things, a week for others and a month for special items; but a year is still quite meaningless when it comes to mitigating want, and the present reality retains a quality of absoluteness that will give way, only after a great deal more experience, to a sense of the relative nature of events to one's time-scale. Only at the age of forty or fifty do most people have any sort of perspective on a day or a month in the context of a lifetime, while only a few gurus and octogenarians are able to appreciate the relationships of moments or lifetimes to eternity (by fully realizing the irrelevance of the arbitrary concept of time).

The infant (like the enlightened guru) lives in the eternal now, the infant in arms (and the guru) in a state of bliss, the infant *out* of arms in a state of longing in the bleakness of an empty universe. His expectations are mingling with actuality, and the innate, ancestral expectations are being overlaid (not altered or replaced) by those based upon his own experience. The amounts by which the two sets of expectations diverge determine the distance that will separate him from his inherent potential for well-being.

The two sets of expectations are not at all similar. The evolved ones are in the nature of certainties until they are betrayed, while the learned ones which deviate from them have the negative character of disillusionment and manifest themselves as doubt, suspicion, fear of being wounded by further experience or, most irreversible of all, resignation.

All these responses are continuum protectors in action, but resignation as a result of utter hopelessness serves to numb the original expectation that conditions will be found in which the sequence of expectations and fulfilments may proceed.

Lines of development are halted at the point where their particular requirements for experience cease to be met. Some lines are stopped in infancy, while others go on to be arrested at a later time in childhood or continue to develop through adulthood as they have evolved to do. Aspects of emotional, intellectual and physical faculties may coexist but be at widely disparate stages of maturity in deprived individuals. All the developmental lines, stunted or matured, go on working together as they are, each waiting for the experience which can fulfil its need, unable to go ahead on anything else. Well-being depends very much upon *how* functioning is limited and in which aspects.

At birth, then, there are shocks that do not shock, either because they are expected (and would be missed) or because they do not happen all at once. Birth cannot correctly be thought of as marking the baby's completion, like the end of an assembly line, for some complements have already been 'born' in the womb and others will not become operative until later. Fresh from a series of expectations and their fulfilments in the womb, the newborn infant would be expectant or, more accurately, certain that his next requirements will also be met.

What happens next? Through tens of millions of generations, what happens is the momentous transfer from the entirely alive surrounding inside the mother's body to a partly live one outside it. Though her all-giving body is there and (ever since the hand-freeing advent of walking erect) her supporting arms as well, there is a great deal of lifeless, alien air touching the infant's body. But he is ready for that too; his place in arms is the expected place, known to his inmost sense as *his* place, and what he experiences while he is in arms is acceptable to his continuum, fulfils his current needs and contributes correctly to his development.

Again, the quality of his awareness is very different from what it will become. He cannot qualify his impression of how things are. They are either right or not right. Requirements are strict at this early date. As we have seen, he cannot hope, if he is uncomfortable now, that he will be comfortable later. He cannot feel that 'mother will be right back' when she leaves him; the world has suddenly gone wrong; conditions are intolerable. He hears and accepts his own weeping, but although his mother knows the sound and its meaning since time immemorial, and so does any child or adult who hears it, he does not. He senses only that it is a positive action towards setting things right. But if he is left to cry too long, if the response it is meant to elicit does not come, that feeling departs as well, giving way to utter bleakness without time or hope. When his mother does come to him, he simply feels right; he is not aware that she has been away, nor does he remember having cried. He is reconnected to his lifeline, and his environment meets his expectations. When he is abandoned, put out of his continuum of correct experience, nothing is acceptable and nothing accepted. Want is all there is; there is nothing to use, to grow on, to fulfil his requirement for experience, for the experiences must be the expected ones, and nothing in his evolving ancestors' experience has prepared him to be left alone, asleep or awake, and even less to cry without a response from any one of his own people.

The feeling appropriate to an infant in arms is his feeling of rightness or essential goodness. The only positive identity he can know being the animal he is, is based on the premise that he is right, good and welcome. Without that conviction, a human being of any age is crippled by a lack of confidence, of a full sense of self, of spontaneity, of grace. All babies are good but can know it themselves only by reflection, by the way they are treated. There is no other visible way for a human being to feel about himself; all other kinds of feeling are unusable as a foundation for well-being. *Rightness is the basic feeling about self that is appropriate to the individuals of our species.* Behaviour not conditioned by a sense of one's own essential rightness will not be the behaviour for which we are evolved and therefore not only will waste millions of years of perfecting but also cannot be well suited to any of our relationships in the self or outside it. Without the sense of being right, one has no sense of how much one ought to claim of comfort, security, help, companionship, love, friendship, things, pleasure or joy. A person without this sense often feels there is an empty space where he ought to be.

Many a life is spent in seeking nothing much more than proof that one exists. Racing-car drivers, mountain climbers, war heroes and other daredevils who flirt with death by predilection are often only trying to feel, by contrasting it as closely as they can with its opposite, that they are, in fact, alive. But shaking up the instinct for self-preservation can only dimly and temporarily simulate the steady, warm current of the missing sense of self.

The attractiveness of babies and children is necessarily a powerful force; without it they would have no advantage to compensate for their many disadvantages as small, weak, slow, defenceless, inexperienced and dependent individuals among their elders. Their appeal precludes their having to compete and attracts the assistance they require.

So strong are the tenderness triggers in babies, that they work across the borders between species as nothing else does. A baby animal awakens a maternal response in all of us, men, women and children; we want to cuddle and give it things, protect and care for it, whether it is a newly born walrus, a baby elephant, a tiger cub or a day-old mouse. The signals are there: the dewy helplessness, the extra-soft hair, fur or feathers, the head larger in proportion to the body than the adult's, the ill-coordinated eagerness and the indiscriminate trust. And in each of us there is the responding mechanism that turns us instantly tender and desirous of lending our services to the little animal's purposes, even if one purpose is to grow big and strong and become our natural enemy.

Conversely, a human baby gives its tenderizing cues to a ravening wolf pack and is carried to their den, kept warm and given wolf's milk despite having poked the mother wolf in the eye, pushed her cubs aside and pulled the father's tail. Big dogs and small cats take the maternal, all-tolerant role with human babies and each other's babies, and would no doubt have an equally workable exchange understanding with infant aardvarks if the situation arose. Primitive hunters often kill an animal for food and bring the victim's orphan home to be suckled by their delighted wives.

It is well to make clear that the maternal role does not have to be taken by the baby's biological mother to fulfil his needs. Nor does the mother surrogate have to be either female or adult, except at feeding time, and even then not even of the same species, for milk, unlike the rest of each species' diet, can be used fairly interchangeably among us all. In this, one can sense the mammal continuum at work, subordinating the disparateness of genera and species to its priorities, obviously not only for the purpose of cross-specific feeding but also because the mammalian prototype that we each have been before developing along our own lines is so quintessential a determinant of our respective natures. In fact, the maternal–filial relationship, that long precedes the advent of mammals on earth rings responsive bells in us, as well as the signals given by non-mammal animals in diminishing degrees according to the time since we have parted company with their kind. Thus we are quite urgently affected by a fuzzy yellow duckling or chick but less so by a baby turtle, even less by a new-born fish, much less by the offspring of a grasshopper, almost imperceptibly by a worm-child or sea-urchin and not at all by a newly kicked-off amoeba, should we catch sight of one through a microscope. We are not simply amused but deeply pleased by the sight of one species caring for the young of another. It appeals to our continuum sense of good practice and therefore registers at the physical level as pleasure.

Walt Disney built an empire on infantile tenderness cues. He avoided human babies almost entirely, perhaps because babies 'belonging' to, or being looked after by, someone else trigger a hands-off mechanism in us that except in pathological cases, inhibits strong impulses to interfere. But he endowed his animals generously with the human infant's appeal signals – fat cheeks, extra-large head in proportion to body (which most baby animals also have to a somewhat lesser degree) and wide eyes with little spiky lashes sweeping up from the outer corners. There were also the small nose and the little mouth crowded by the cheeks and the unruly softness and cowlicks of the hair, often translated into representations of animals which, though appealing for the downiness of their fur, do not actually have cowlicks.

In the film *Pinocchio* the marionette hero was just far enough from human to enjoy the advantages of all the cue-laden inventiveness of the masters at Walt Disney Studios, but when he turned into a real boy he had to give up many of the exaggerated signals to avoid looking monstrous to the viewers' sense of how a little boy (no longer a baby) should look.

Dumbo, the baby elephant protagonist of another film, had almost all the cues in flagrant proportions – enormous head, great trusting eyes with the requisite lashes at the corners, bad coordination, eagerness – and his nose was as small as an elephant representation could possibly sustain.

Bambi conformed more to the high-appeal cues of a real fawn, with long, wobbly, knock-kneed legs and high, round little rump, sudden alert head movements and solemn but shakily coordinated efforts to behave like a grown-up deer, but his eyes and lashes were humanized, as were many of his movements and expressions, trading, as it were, on the best of both worlds. Supporting ducks, chipmunks, rabbits, birds, kittens, skunks, goldfish and not-quite-human specimens such as the seven dwarves were all given the irresistible cues, and the villains, witches, wicked stepmothers, cruel puppet masters and so on were equally exaggeratedly deprived of them and furnished with strict or stringy hair, large bony noses, small eyes and small heads. (The ones who had to be human and attractive but not infantile, like Snow White, the Prince, and Cinderella and her Prince, were all devoid of the Disney power and looked decidedly wishy-washy among the emotion-tugging cue-bearers. If *their* appropriate appeal cues, which at their age are sexually associated ones, had been exploited in the same manner, Uncle Walt might, in that era, have found himself in court.)

The maternal role, the only role that can relate to an infant in the earliest months, is instinctively played by fathers, other children and anyone else who deals with the infant, even for a moment. Distinguishing between sex or age groups is not the business of a baby.

The irrelevance of masculine or feminine characteristics to the maternal or paternal role has been demonstrated by experiments in a French psychiatric clinic, where women doctors were father figures to their patients while male nurses, in their capacity as everyday carers for the patients, became equally satisfactory mother figures. (This is the sort of thing the intellect suddenly discovers after man has been acting upon it instinctively for several millions of years.)

So there is for an infant one possible kind of relationship, and in each of us resides a full set of responses to his cues. We also, every man, woman, girl and boy of us, possess a minutely detailed knowledge of baby-care technique, notwithstanding the fact that lately (by which I mean for no more than a few thousand years) we have allowed the intellect to try out its gauche fads on this most critical matter and have trespassed against our inbuilt ability so capriciously that its very existence is by now all but forgotten.

It is standard practice in the 'advanced' countries to buy a book on baby care the moment a new arrival is expected. It may be the current fashion to let the baby cry until its heart is broken and it gives up, goes numb and becomes a 'good baby', or to pick it up when the mother feels like it and has nothing else to do at that moment, or, as one recent school of thought had it, to leave the baby in an emotional vacuum, untouched except for absolute necessity and then shown no facial expression, no pleasure, no smiles, no admiration, only a blank stare. Whatever it is, young mothers read and obey, untrusting of their innate ability, untrusting of the baby's 'motives' in giving the still perfectly clear signals. Babies have, indeed, become a sort of enemy to be vanquished by the mother. Crying must be ignored so as to show the baby who is boss, and a basic premise in the relationship is that every effort should be made to force the baby to conform to the mother's wishes. Displeasure, disapproval or some other sign of a withdrawal of love is shown when the baby's behaviour causes 'work', 'wastes' time or is otherwise deemed inconvenient. The notion is that catering to the desires of a baby will 'spoil' him and going counter to them will serve to tame, or socialize, him. In reality, the opposite effect is obtained in either case.

The period immediately following birth is the most impressive part of life outside the mother's body. What a baby encounters is what he feels the nature of life to be. Each later impression can only qualify, to a greater or lesser degree, the first impression, made when he had no previous data about the external world. His expectations are the most inflexible he will ever have. The change from the total hospitality of the womb is enormous, but, as we have seen, he has come prepared for the great leap from the womb to his place in arms.

What he has not come prepared for is a greater leap of any sort, let alone a leap into nothingness, non-life, a basket with cloth in it or a plastic box without motion, sound, odour or the feel of life. The violent tearing apart of the mother–child continuum, so strongly established during the phases that took place in the womb, may understandably result in depression for the mother as well as agony for the infant.

Every nerve ending under his newly exposed skin craves the expected embrace; all his being, the character of all he is, leads to his being held in arms. For millions of years newborn babies have been held close to their mothers from the moment of birth. Some babies of the last few hundred generations have been deprived of this all-important experience, but that has not lessened each new baby's expectation that *he* will be in his rightful place. When our antecedents went about on all fours and had fur to cling to, it was the babies who kept the mother–child bond intact. Their survival depended upon it. As we became hairless and stood up on our hind legs, freeing the mother's hands, it became incumbent upon her to keep her and her child together. That she has recently, in some places in the world, taken her responsibility to maintain their contact to be a matter of option does not alter in the least the powerful urgency of the baby's need to be held.

She herself is being deprived of a precious part of her own expected life experience, the enjoyment of which would have encouraged her to continue to behave as is most rewarding both to herself and her baby.

The state of consciousness of an infant changes enormously during the in-arms phase. At the beginning he is more like other animals than he is like an adult human. Step by step, as his central nervous system develops, he becomes more particularly *Homo sapiens*. Experience does not simply impress him more or less but in different ways altogether, as his faculties increase in number as well as in acuity. The earliest established components of an infant's psycho-biological make-up are those most formative of his lifelong outlook. What he feels before he can think is a powerful determinant of what kind of things he thinks when thought becomes possible.

If he feels safe, wanted and 'at home' in the midst of activity before he can think, his view of later experiences will be very distinct in character from those of a child who feels unwelcome, unstimulated by the experiences he has missed and accustomed to living in a state of want, though the later experiences of both may be identical.

At first the infant only notices; he cannot reason. He becomes familiar with his surroundings by association. At the very outset, in the first post-natal messages brought in by the senses, there is an absoluteness, an unqualified impression of the state of things, relative to nothing but the innate expectations of the infant and, of course, devoid of any relation to the passage of time. If the continuum did not operate in this way, the shock of novel events to the new organism would be intolerable. What is noticeable, at the beginning of an infant's ability to pay attention to events outside himself, is the difference between what is sensed and what it resembles in his previous experience. Learning the world by association means that he takes in whole what he has never known before, without 'noticing' anything about it. Note is paid only to similar but partly differing later experiences, so that the world is learned first grossly, then in finer and finer detail.

In this respect *Homo sapiens* is unique among animals. His expectation is to find a suitable environment, learn it more and more precisely and act upon it with increasing efficiency. Other primates, in varying degrees, adapt to *some* circumstances as they encounter them, but animals are predominantly designed (evolved) to behave according to innate patterns.

A giant anteater cub I acquired when he was four days old grew up happily in human society and clearly regarded us all as anteaters and expected us to behave appropriately, prancing and sparring with him in a manner traditional to anteaters. I, as his mother, was expected to remain in communication with him at all times, but at increasing distances, as he grew more self-reliant; to carry him about at first, then allow him to hug me as often as the spirit required and to lick my toes with great frequency; to keep him company while he ate; and to come when he called after having strayed out of smelling range. But he looked upon dogs and horses as enemies, not of his species.

A woolly monkey, which I also brought up from infancy, on the contrary, appeared to think of herself as a person. She treated dogs, even large ones, with condescension and was known to take a chair in a group of seated people while the dogs, bamboozled by her imperious conduct (though they would have chased a cat twice her size), lay faithfully at her feet. She learned polite table manners and, after observing for about a year, learned to open a door by climbing the jamb and then simultaneously turning the door knob counterclockwise and pulling.

Her behaviour patterns therefore comprised a greater proportion of adaptiveness, of expectation to learn from personal experience, than the anteater's, whose behaviour was almost entirely pre-set by innate mechanisms.

Man, more adaptive still to his own experience, can cope with variations in his surroundings that would extinguish a less ingenious species. Given a problem, he has a wide choice of reactions. A monkey has relatively little margin within which to respond to a stimulus; an anteater has no choice at all and therefore, as the form he is, is infallible. A monkey can make few mistakes, from the continuum standpoint, but a man is given great vulnerability with his ability to choose.

But along with the widening of man's choice of behaviours, with the increase in his fallibility, there has also evolved the continuum sense that disposes him to choose suitably, so that given the sort of experience needed to develop them and the kind of environment in which he may exercise them, his choices can be almost as infallible as an anteater's.

Human children brought up by animals show, even more revealingly, the importance of an appropriate environment in attaining a species' evolved expectations.

Of the many cases on record, perhaps the best documented is the story of Amala and her sister Kamala, who were cared for from babyhood by wolves in the jungles of India. When found, they were taken to an orphanage where a Reverend and Mrs Singh attempted to educate them into human society. Most of the Singhs' painstaking efforts met with failure or only slight success. The girls were miserable and lay naked, in a position appropriate to wolves, in the corners of their rooms. They became active at night and howled to attract the attention of their old wolf pack. After a great deal of training, Kamala learned to walk on two legs, but could never run except on all fours. They refused to wear clothes for some time or to eat cooked food, preferring raw meat and carrion. Kamala learned fifty words before she died at the age of fifteen. Her mental age at the time was estimated at three and a half by human standards.

The ability to adapt to conditions unsuited to their species of children who have grown up among animals is far greater than the ability of any animal to adapt to human ways. But the early death of most of the children, the suffering they endure after capture and their inability to superimpose a human culture upon their established and developed animal cultures also show the profundity with which the culture, once learned, is rendered part of the nature of the human individual. *The expectation of taking part in a culture is a product of our evolution, and the mores that are seized upon by that expectation are, when assimilated, as integral a component of our personalities as the inborn ways of other species.* The children of the wild therefore, being human and subject to greater influence from their own experience than any animal, have been so thoroughly cultivated in another animal's behaviour that they have shown far greater stress as a result of changing their environment than an animal would, fortified to a much higher degree as animals are by innate (uninfluenceable) behaviour patterns.

That Kamala's mental age was so low is a meaningless factor viewed alone, but, seen as part of the continuum of a creature born human and reared as a wolf, it may very well represent the optimum use of a good mind in the circumstances. Some of her abilities were prodigious: her agility as a quadruped, her sense of smell (she was able to smell meat at eighty yards), her night vision, her speed, her adaptability to changes in temperature. Her judgement in hunting and her sense of direction must have been extraordinary as well to have enabled her to survive as a wolf. In sum, her continuum served her well. She developed from her potential what she needed for her way of life. That she could not undo her development and replace it with a completely new one is insignificant; there is no reason why any creature need be adaptable to such an improbable exigency. No more could a grown human be expected to adapt successfully as another animal when his behaviour is already conditioned to human society.

From the beginning learning is selective; it is always relevant to what is known subjectively about the life to be led. The associative process ensures that. Like a radio, set to receive only selected wavelengths on a receiver capable of receiving many more and different wavelengths, the psycho-biological receptor starts with a vast potential and is soon set to the required ranges. The optimum range of vision for most human ways of life is limited to daylight and a degree of night vision and to the spectrum of colours between red and purple. Those things that are too small or too distant are eliminated from our perceptions, and of the things within range only a limited number can be seen sharply. In the middle distance, where it is useful to see what is happening on all sides, vision is sharp. When something or someone of interest approaches, peripheral vision blurs accordingly until the object is within a short distance. The middle distance is put out of focus, and attention is directed more effectively to the nearby object, the better to deal with it undistracted. If everything around the object remained equally sharp, the burden upon the senses would be greater and would impede the brain, which must direct its attention to the single object, or an aspect of the object, for utmost efficiency. According to the culture, ranges are selected for the vision of the individual, within, of course, the boundaries of his evolved nature.

Children raised by wolves are reported to have extraordinary night vision. The Yequana can select the form of a small bird in the shadows of a wall of jungle where one of us can see only leaves, even after they have pointed to the place. They can see a fish amid the foaming waters of a rapids, again invisible to the most concentrated attempts of our eyes.

Hearing, too, is selective – limited to what our culture tells us is relevant, eliminative of the rest. The auditory mechanism itself is capable of hearing far more than we use it to hear. All the South American Indians I have known, accustomed to listening for both dangers and game in jungles that could hide them from sight within a few feet, can also hear the approach of an outboard motor or an aeroplane long before any one of us.

Their range suits their needs. Ours serve our purposes better, weeding out what to our lives would, more often than not, be pointless noise. There is nothing in our culture that would make it more than a hindrance, for example, to be awakened by the sound of grunting two hundred yards away.

To prevent the mind from being flooded with unedited sensations, the nervous system itself serves as editor. Attention to sounds can be phased in and out, not at will but according to the conditioning of the editing mechanism. Though the hearing apparatus cannot be turned off, some audible sounds are never heard by the conscious mind but remain subliminal from babyhood to death. A classic demonstration used by stage hypnotists is one in which a subject is commanded to hear what is being whispered at what seems an impossible distance. The hypnotist substitutes his selection for the subject's normal range. He succeeds in giving the illusion that he is heightening the power of the ear, when in fact he is suspending the editing out of sounds at the unused end of the ear's range.

Powers called supernatural or magical are often only ones that are not selected by the nervous system (at the behest of the continuum) as appropriate to enter our range of faculties. They can be cultivated by disciplines that overcome the normal process of elimination, or they can appear under duress, as in the case of a ten-year-old boy whose brother was pinned under a fallen tree. Terrified, he lifted the tree off his brother's body before running for help. It was later found that a dozen men were required to move the trunk that the boy, in his extraordinary emotional state, had lifted alone. Stories of this kind are many. The powers they describe are liberated only for special circumstances.

Interesting exceptions to this rule are individuals whose editing mechanisms have somehow been damaged, either temporarily or permanently, and who have become clairvoyant. I do not pretend to know how this works, but some have the ability to see underground water or metals. Others can see auras around people. Peter Hurkos, the famous American clairvoyant, became one after injuring his head in a fall from a ladder. Two friends of mine told me in confidence of their horrifying ability to see into the future while they neared nervous breakdowns. The stories were told me separately, and the girls did not know each other, but they were both hospitalized a few days after the clairvoyant episodes, which did not recur. If the normal limits of human ability are broken, it is usually when emotions are strained to their limits. In accidents, when the victim is confronted without warning by the imminence of his own death, he reaches out in his helplessness to his mother or whoever occupies the maternal position for him. Frequently the mother, or mother figure, receives the message, no matter what the distance. The situation arises sufficiently often for most of us to have known or heard of cases ourselves.

Premonition works the other way; an unknowable event that threatens extreme consequences can break through into the consciousness of someone quite calm, either dreaming or awake. A great deal of premonition goes unheeded and, due to prohibitions against belief in 'such things', is often unrecognized. A vague statement like 'I had a feeling I shouldn't have come' is usually the only acknowledgement of a premonition that was overruled by other pressures.

How events that appear not yet to have occurred can be perceived – in what way they can exist before happening – I have not a clue. But then past and present events known without recourse to the senses are mechanically just as mysterious. And many other means of communication, like the signals given by recently discovered chemical substances that compel specific behaviour in animals and the pinpoint direction finders in migrating birds, are equally beyond our ken.

The conscious mind is not what it seems to itself to be, nor does it have access to the programming secrets of the continuum it is evolved to serve. *To make of the intellect a competent servant instead of an incompetent master must be a major goal of continuum philosophy.* Used correctly, the intellect can be an invaluable asset. In perceiving, classifying and comprehending the relationships and characteristics of the animals, vegetables, minerals and events they encounter, human intellects can make, store and transmit to one another vast bodies of information that render the environment useful in a far more inclusive and flexible way than could be accomplished by any other animal. This reduces man's vulnerability to the vicissitudes of that environment. He has more alternatives available in his behaviour towards the elements about him and is therefore more stable in his position among them.

With the natural balance unimpaired, the intellect is capable of serving as a protector of the continuum as it becomes aware of the dictates of the continuum sense and acts upon them appropriately. Reason, judgement based upon personal experience and the communicated experience of others, and the ability to synthesize thoughts and memories in an infinity of useful combinations by induction and by deduction, add to its value in serving the individual's and the species' best interests.

Bent upon the task of acquainting itself with every aspect of botany, for example, an intellect in harmony with a fully developed and soundly working continuum sense can take in seemingly prodigious amounts of information. Reports from observers of many primitive cultures concur that every man, woman and child in each society has a highly detailed catalogue in his head of the names and characteristics of hundreds or thousands of plants.

One such observer, E. Smith-Bowen, speaking of an African tribe and the enormous knowledge of botany shared by every member, said, 'None of them would ever believe that I am incapable of knowing as much as they, even if I wanted to do so.'*

I do not mean to imply that the savage is innately more intelligent than we, but I do believe that the natural potential of the mind can be damaged by pressures from a distorted personality.

In a fulfilled member of a society which expects it of him, an intellect can memorize an incredible amount of information and retain it for use. Even among the civilized, illiterates, who do not expect most of the responsibility for storing information to be left to books as we do, can be seen to have more highly developed memories, but they might have even more if they were fully at peace with themselves and their world.

The conditioning of the infant mind is the main determinant of the character of the ranges selected for use in his life. He expects to be cued by his experiences, and he expects a great quantity and variety of cues. Further, he expects that the experiences that cue him will have a direct and usable bearing upon the situations he will encounter later in life.

When his later experiences do not correspond in character to the ones that conditioned him, he tends to influence them to acquire that character, for better or for worse. If he is accustomed to loneliness, he will unconsciously arrange his affairs to assure him a similar level of loneliness. Attempts on his own part, or of circumstances, to make him very much more or less lonely than is customary to him will be resisted by his tendency towards stability.

Even a customary degree of anxiety tends to be maintained, for the sudden loss of 'anything to worry about' can cause a far more profound and infinitely more acute form of anxiety. For someone whose natural habitat is the brink of disaster, a giant step into security is as intolerable as the realization of all he most fears. At work is the tendency to maintain what should have been the high level of well-being established in babyhood.

---

*E. Smith-Bowen, *Return to Laughter*, London, 1954.

Radical changes in one's measure of success or failure, happiness or unhappiness and wholesale changes in one's established associations, are resisted by our in-built stabilizers, and we often find ourselves pitting our wills against them. The will is seldom of much effect against the power of 'habit'. But sometimes changes are forced upon an individual by external events. The stabilizers then produce balances for situations that cannot be assimilated as they are. Distractions such as demanding (but familiar) problems may take the edge off an intolerable success or failure.

To make the adaptation required by an irreversible change, after every effort has failed to restore the *status quo*, one must often retire from combat, slip into neutral gear and reorient oneself to the new circumstances that life has dictated. This sometimes requires an illness or an accident that immobilizes the victim long enough to rest and realign his forces to suit the new requirements. The tendency to stabilize also uses the body to restore balance by allowing it to succumb to illness when there is an emotional need for 'babying' and a potential motherer available. It brings on a cold, when a short trip *hors de combat* will suffice a person pushed too far from the amount of well-being in which he feels at home or when he is called upon to stretch his usual behaviour too far.

To make life tolerable, some human beings must be in a dire physical state with enormous frequency (the accident-prone), and some must be stricken permanently in order to survive in the presence of their need for mothering, distraction or punishment, as the case may be. Others must develop a state of fragility to maintain their families in necessary relationships towards them, actually becoming ill only when treated too badly, or too well, by the others concerned.

Among my acquaintances perhaps the most extreme case of the use of illness to supply stability was a woman in whom a near-unbearable burden of guilt was the troubling factor.

The nature of my friend's early treatment, the incontrovertible evidence to her infant mind that she was 'bad', is unknown to me and probably to her as well, but her twin brother, who must have shared her torment, committed suicide when he was twenty-one. With the added weight of guilt, albeit irrational, which inevitably accompanies the death of a sibling of a deprived person, doubled perhaps by the extra closeness of twins, she set about finding suitable punishments to balance it all off to a point at which she could live with it. The stabilizing mechanism of her battered continuum, taking its method and detail from her culture, had to reduce the danger of her having a 'successful' life, over, as it were, her brother's dead body. Her conditioning, the guilt of babyhood, repressed and later slashed open by her brother's suicide, could not have tolerated any measure of good fortune for herself.

Within a few years she had had two illegitimate children, one by a man of another race, the other by an unknown man. She had taken several jobs that were, for her social background, humiliating; she contracted poliomyelitis and thus became confined to a wheelchair for the rest of her life; she caught tuberculosis while in the hospital for polio, ruining one lung and seriously damaging the other; she dyed her hair an extremely unbecoming purplish red, which went far towards spoiling her persistent prettiness; and she took up residence with a failed artist far older than herself.

When I last heard from her she told me with her usual gaiety that she had been clearing up after a party, had fallen out of her wheelchair, and had broken one of her paralysed legs.

She was never gloomy and never complained; she grew visibly more cheerful as disaster followed upon disaster, relieving her of her inner burden more and more efficiently. I asked her once whether I were imagining it or if it were true that she was happier since becoming crippled. She answered immediately that she had never been happier in her life.

Half a dozen similar cases come to mind. Several are men who grew beards or acquired scars to disguise physical attractiveness that made life uncomfortably easy and women more loving towards them than they could reconcile with their feelings of unlovableness.

There are both men and women who can be attracted only to people who could not possibly be interested in them.

Failures of every sort are usually traceable not to lack of ability, not to bad luck, not to competition, but to a tendency in the subject to maintain the condition in which he has learned to feel at home.

So when an infant forms an impression of his relationship to all that is other than himself, he is building the belief framework that will become his home for life, to which everything will be referred, by which everything will be measured and balanced. His stabilizing mechanisms will be at work to maintain it. A baby deprived of the experience necessary to give him the basis for full flowering of his innate potential will perhaps never know a moment of the sense of unconditional rightness that has been natural to his kind for 99.99 per cent of its history. Deprivation, in the degree to which he has suffered its discomfort and limitations in infancy, will be maintained indiscriminately as part of his development. Instinctive forces do not reason. They assume, from the immense weight of their experience of nature's ways, that it will serve the individual well to be stabilized according to his initial experience.

That this aid could become a cruel trap, a sort of life sentence in a portable prison, is an eventuality so remote to the evolutionary process, so recent in animal history, that few provisions are found in our natures to alleviate the pain. There are some. There are neuroses and insanities to protect the deprived from the full brunt of unmeetable reality. There is a numbness that overtakes pain beyond bearing. Death lets out others, most commonly those whose strong infantile need for a maternal figure has followed them into middle or old age, when the person who plays that role for them withdraws through dying, running off with a secretary or whatever, leaving the dependent person bereft of any hope of finding a new support and unable to live with the emptiness inside as well as out to which the missing person lent a presence.

To a person with a fully enriched infancy, who is therefore enrichable by his ongoing life, the loss of a longtime mate is not equal to loss of 'everything' at any age. His or her self is not an empty vessel dependent upon someone else for substance or motivation. The wholly adult self will grieve and regroup its forces to accommodate the change, perhaps during a period of retreat.

In evolved cultures, and in many civilized ones as well, there are ritual aids to the process of grieving (communal lamenting, ceremonies, gatherings); especially when the culture does not comprise an exact procedure for the survivor's new life, nor is it dictated by the continuing requirements of children or other dependents, there is often an allotment of time for redirectioning which is supported by the society. The wearing of black or white, or some other sign of being out of play (out of the colours of life, as it were), marks the spirit in chrysalis and asks for the recognition of society and its indulgence.

That the civilized intellect has seized upon and diminished the functioning of these mores from their evolved forms into grotesque exaggerations uncorrelated to the real need, or wiped them out entirely, does not alter the integrity and wholesomeness of their origins. Nor do continuum stabilizers neglect to fill the need for members of cultures with inadequate or absent provisions for grief. As for all parallel exigencies, it produces shelter, often in the form of illness or accident, if no better opportunity for a rehabilitation period presents itself.

The extent of the wrench caused by a change in a person's environment depends, of course, upon the extent to which he has been able to develop his innate potential for resilience, and the measure of repair follows accordingly.

How can we learn about continuum and non-continuum infant life? We can make a start by observing people like the Yequana and look again more carefully at members of our own cultures. The worlds of infants in arms in Stone Age and in civilized cultures are as different as day and night.

From birth, continuum infants are taken everywhere. Before the umbilicus comes off, the infant's life is already full of action. He is asleep most of the time, but even as he sleeps he is becoming accustomed to the voices of his people, to the sounds of their activities, to the bumpings, jostlings and moves without warning, to stops without warning, to lifts and pressures on various parts of his body as his caretaker shifts him about to accommodate her work or her comfort, and to the rhythms of day and night, the changes of texture and temperature on his skin and the safe, right feel of being held to a living body. His urgent need to be there would be noticeable to him only if he were removed from his place. His unequivocal expectation of these circumstances, and the fact that these and no other are his experience, simply carry on the continuum of his species. He is feeling right, therefore he seldom has any need to signal by crying or to do anything but suckle when the impulse arises and enjoy satisfying the stimulus to do so, and equally to enjoy the stimulus and satisfaction of defecating. Otherwise he is engaged in learning what it is like to be.

During the in-arms phase, the time between birth and the voluntary commencement of crawling, a baby is receiving experience and with it fulfilling his innate expectations, graduating to new expectations or desires and then fulfilling them in their turn. He moves very little when he is awake and is generally in a relaxed and passive state. His muscles have tone; he is not in the rag-doll condition in which he sleeps, but he uses only the economical minimum of muscular activity needed to pay attention to the events that concern him at each stage, to eat and to defecate. He also has the task, which falls to him fairly early, though not immediately after birth, of balancing his head and body (for paying attention, eating and defecating) in an infinite variety of postures depending upon the actions and positions of the person holding him.

He may be lying on a lap in only occasional contact with arms and hands that are working at something above him, like paddling a canoe, sewing or preparing food. Then he might suddenly feel the lap tilting him outward and a hand gripping his wrist. The lap drops away and the hand tightens its grip and lifts him through the air to a new contact with the trunk of the body, whereupon the hand lets go and an elbow takes up a supporting position by pinning him against a hip and rib cage before bending to pick something up with the free hand, upending him momentarily then proceeding to walk, run, then walk again, bobbing him up and down in several rhythms and giving him a variety of jolts. He may then be passed to someone else and feel himself losing contact with one person and coming into the new temperature, texture, smell and sound of another, a bonier one perhaps, or one with the reedy voice of a child or the resonance of a man's. Or he may be lifted again by one arm and dunked into cool water, splashed and stroked, then scraped with the side of a hand until the water stops trickling down his body. He may then be replaced, damp on damp, in his place on the hip until the contact area generates great heat while the areas exposed to air grow colder. He may then feel the sun's warmth come through, or the extra chill of a breeze. He may feel both, as he is taken through sunshine to the shade of a forest path. He may be almost dry, then drenched by pelting rain, and later refind comfort in a radical change from cold and wet to shelter and a fire at his outer side, which warms him faster than his other side is being warmed by his companion's body.

If there is a party while he is asleep, he will be bounced about quite violently while his mother hops and stamps in time to the music. Through daytime sleep, similar adventures befall him. At night his mother sleeps beside him, her skin next to his, as always, while she breathes and moves and sometimes snores a little. She wakens often during the night to tend the fire, holding him close as she rolls out of her hammock and slips to the floor, where he is sandwiched between her thigh and ribs as she rearranges the logs. If he awakens hungry in the night he signals with a soft grunt if he cannot find her breast; she will then give it to him, and again his well-being will be re-established, without ever having come near to straining the limits of his continuum. His life, full of action, is consistent with the lives lived by millions of his predecessors and meets the expectations of his nature.

He does very little, then, at this stage, but a great quantity and variety of experience come to him through his adventures in the arms of a busy person. As his requirements change, when the preceding ones have been satisfactorily met and he is psychologically developed and ready for the next ones, he signals, according to his innate impulses, and the signals are correctly interpreted by the corresponding innate mechanisms in his beholders. When he smiles and gurgles, it excites pleasure in them and an impulse to elicit the delightful sounds as long and often as possible. The right stimuli are quickly identified and, encouraged by the rewarding response of the baby, repeated. Later, as the level of pleasure and excitement diminishes with repetition, his cues and responses push the behaviour pattern to alter in the direction that will sustain the high pleasure quotient.

Games of approach and retreat are examples of this. They may begin with an affectionate kiss on the infant's face or body. He smiles and gurgles. Another kiss follows. More signs of pleasure and encouragement come from the baby. The tone of his happy voice and the sparkle in his eyes do not signal for peace and quiet, nor for comforting, nor for feeding or repositioning, but for excitement. Instinctively, his accomplice rubs her nose on his chest and when this meets with success, she very soon creates even more gleeful signals with a vibrating b-b-b-b-b-b from lips brushing the surface of his body.

The infant, anticipating his own reaction, now starts gurgling and squealing with excitement as the pleasure-giving mouth approaches. The man, woman or child who owns the mouth finds that the rewarding sounds from the baby can be increased by teasing, that is, delaying the approach to the point where maximum effect is maintained: not too long for the baby to remain attentive, nor too short a time to obtain all the anticipatory response possible.

The next step in the game is to hold the baby at arm's length and then pull him into the close contact, or safe, position. The contrast between the fringe zone and safety zone, the relationship between moving outward and coming back unharmed, the triumph of having tested one's own separability from the safety zone and returning successful, is the beginning of the progression of events and psychobiological maturing that will lead to graduation from the in-arms phase with maximum competence and eagerness for the next adventures on the age-old agenda.

As the arm's-length position is tried and mastered, a toss with a loosening of the grip at the zenith follows. When the infant shows that he is ready for something more daring, he is thrown and caught. He is allowed to fly higher and drop further as his confidence increases, as the borderline at which he exhibits fear is pushed back and his radius of confidence expands.

Games that test the same qualities in the context of the separate senses are also learned from infants by their companions. The reassuring sight of a mother or familiar is cut off and restored in the same progressive way in games of peek-a-boo. Increasingly sudden or loud sounds are sprung upon the infant's ear – as, for example, 'Boo!' – followed by the reassuring news that it is only Mummy or whoever, and there is no cause for alarm. Toys of the jack-in-the-box kind remove the startling stimulus to the world outside and test greater degrees of resilience. There can be games that follow the pattern but are initiated by the adult. The Yequana take advantage of the baby's predisposition to this sort of performance and, keeping his rules and respecting his go-ahead signals, dip him into more and more challenging waters. A daily bath is routine from birth, but every infant is also dipped into fast rivers, first only his feet, then his legs, then his entire body. The water goes from swift to swifter and on to plunging rapids and falls, and the time of exposure lengthens too, as the baby's response reveals growing confidence. Before he can walk or even think, a Yequana baby is well on the way towards expertise in judging the force, direction and depth of water by sight. His people are among the finest white-water canoeists in the world.

The senses are given an enormous quantity and variety of events and objects upon which to practise, refine their functions and coordinate their messages to the brain.

The first experiences are predominantly of the body of a busy mother. The movings about are bases for taking up the pace of an active life. The pace becomes a characteristic of the world of living and it is associated always with the cosy rightness of the self, for it is learned in arms.

If a baby is held much of the time by someone who is only sitting quietly, it will not serve him in learning the quality of life and action, though it will keep away negative feelings of abandonment, separateness, and much of the worst torment of longing. The fact that babies actively encourage people to treat them to excitement is indication that they expect and require action upon which to develop. A mother sitting still will condition a baby to think of life as dull and slow, and there will be a restlessness in him and frequent promptings from him to encourage more stimulation. He will bounce up and down to show what he wants, or wave his arms to initiate a faster pace in her actions. Similarly, if she insists upon treating him as though he were fragile, she will suggest to him that he is. But if she handles him in a rough and off-hand way, he will think of himself as strong, adaptable and at home in a vast variety of circumstances. Feeling fragile not only is unpleasant but also interferes with the efficiency of the developing child and, later, of the adult.

The sights, sounds, smells, textures and tastes are first dominated by the sheltering body and later, with the development of greater faculties, include a broadening range of events and objects. Associations are made. The darkness of the hut is always present when there is a smell of cooking and almost always when there is the smell of wood smoke. The light is bright at baths and during most of the joggling of walking trips. The temperature in the dark is more comfortable, generally, than in the bright outdoors, which is often blazingly hot or chilly with wind and rain; but any and all of the changes are acceptable and the variations expected, for there was always variety in babies' experience. The basic condition of being in arms has been met, so the infant is free to be stimulated and enriched by whatever he senses. Happenings that would frighten an unprepared adult are barely noticed by an infant in arms. Figures suddenly loom close above his eyes, treetops spin high overhead. Things go dark or light without warning. Thunder and lightning, barking dogs, deafening roars of waterfalls, splitting trees, flaring fires, surprise dousings in rain or river water do not perturb him. Given the conditions in which his species evolved, silence or a prolonged *lack* of change in sensory stimuli is alarming.

When he does cry for some reason during a moment when a group of adults is in conversation, his mother hisses softly in his ear to distract him. If this fails, she takes him away until he is quiet. She does not set her will against the infant's, she exiles herself with him without showing any sign of judgement of his behaviour or displeasure at being inconvenienced. When he drools on her, she seldom notices. If she wipes his mouth with the back of her hand, it is in the half-attentive manner with which she grooms her own person. When he wets or defecates, she may laugh, and, as she is seldom alone, so do her companions, and she holds the infant away from her as quickly as she can until he finishes. It is a sort of game to see how fast she can hold him away, but the laughter is louder when she gets the worst of it. Water sinks into the dirt floor in moments, and excrement is cleared away immediately with leaves. Vomiting, or 'spitting up', an everyday event in our infants' lives, is so rare that I can remember seeing it happen only once in my years with the Indians, and that baby had a high fever.

The notion that nature has evolved one species to suffer from indigestion every time it drinks its mother's milk has, amazingly, not been questioned by civilized experts. 'Burping', patting the baby firmly on the back while he is held against one's shoulder, is advocated to help him 'bring up the air he has swallowed'. The baby often vomits on the shoulder in the process. Stressed as our babies are, it is little wonder that they are chronically ill. The tension, kicking, arching, flexing and squealing are symptoms of the same constant, deep discomfiture. Yequana babies never require special treatment after nourishing themselves – any more than do the young of other animals. Perhaps part of the explanation lies in the fact that they nurse much more often during the day and night than our civilized babes are permitted to do. It seems more likely, though, that the whole answer rests in our permanently stressed condition, for even when Yequana babies were cared for by children most of the day, and therefore unable to resort to their mothers at will, they showed no sign of colic.*

Later, when house training takes place, the toddler is chased outside if he sullies the hut floor. By that time he is so thoroughly accustomed to feeling and being considered right, or 'good', that his social impulses, as they develop, are harmonious with those of his tribesmen. When an act of his then meets with disapproval, he does not feel it is himself they deplore but his act, and he is motivated to cooperate. There is no impulse to defend himself from them or, in fact, to take any standpoint but theirs; they are his tried and true allies.

This, though it is a terrible irony to have to say so, is what is meant by being a social animal – which brings us to the experiences of non-continuum infants in contemporary Western cultures.

The creature is the same. Though we have a very distinct recent history, our evolutionary history, the millions of formative years that produced the human animal, is common to the Yequana and us alike. The few thousand years that have seen deviation from the continuum lead to civilization have no standing in evolutionary time. In so short a period no significant or noticeable evolving could take place. So the expectations are identical in infants who have come straight down the continuum with no deprived predecessors and those whose births may have been induced to suit the golfing commitments of a suburban obstetrician.

As we have seen, infants of the human species are not less suited than those of any other species to the business of being born. The experiences of birth are part of our repertoire of adaptabilities owing

---

* Dr Frank Lake (see Introduction) told me that his research revealed digestive problems to be the major physical expression of infant stress, while skin problems (eczema, psoriasis, rashes, etc.) were typical results, sometimes much later in life, of distress experienced *in utero*.

to the fact that we have evolved according to the experiences of predecessors, all of whom have been born since the rise of mammals and, before that, hatched, a process that was just as demanding of adaptive resilience. The expected events are those which follow that formative precedent. Unexpected events have no stabilizing mechanisms evolved to assimilate them. There is also a danger that unexpected events at birth will not only accompany but replace the expected ones which are needed for certain lines of development. Little can be found in nature that is wasted. The essence of the evolved system is the economical relatedness of its every aspect functioning as both cause and effect in the developmental process.

This means that deprivation of any well precedented detail of experience will cost the individual some degree of well-being, perhaps one too subtle for us to notice, perhaps one so commonly lost that we do not recognize it as a loss. Research has already shown, as we shall see, that deprivation of the experience of creeping about on hands and knees has deleterious effects upon verbal abilities when they develop at a later stage. It may equally surprisingly turn out that deprivation of being held in a wide variety of positions in infancy, or of being rained on for a given minimum of time, or of experiencing the natural transition of light from day to night, is responsible for deficiency in surefootedness or temperature-variation tolerance or resistance to seasickness later on. A propos surefootedness, a researcher might see if he can isolate something in the experience of Mohawk babies, which does not occur in ours, that accounts for their lack of fear of heights and also the varying degrees in which we are subject to it. (The Yequana, the Sanema and perhaps all tribal South American Indians do not mind heights either, but the Mohawks have many more experiences by now that are learned from us, and the differing ones might be easier to sift in a search for the factor in question.)

Applied to the phenomenon of birth trauma in civilized subjects, continuum principle suggests that contributing causes might be the use of steel instruments, bright lights, rubber gloves, the smell of antiseptic and anaesthetic, loud voices or the sounds of machinery. The baby's experiences during a birth without trauma have to be those, and only those, that correspond to his and his mother's ancient expectations. Many good, sound cultures leave it to the mother to have her baby without any help at all while others, equally sound, prescribe that she be assisted. Either way, the baby is in close contact with his mother's body from the moment he emerges from the womb. When the baby has begun to breathe for himself and is resting serenely on his mother, having been stroked by her until he is calm, and the umbilicus has ceased entirely to pulsate and is then cut, the little creature is given the breast without delay of any sort – for washing, weighing, examining or anything else. It is at this precise time, as soon as the birth is complete, when the mother and baby meet for the first time as separate individuals, that the momentous event of imprinting must take place. It is well known that many little animals are imprinted upon their mothers at birth. Baby geese, as soon as they are hatched, become imprinted on the first nearby object they see moving. It is meant to be their mother, but even if it is a mechanical toy or Konrad Lorenz, they are compelled by their evolved nature to follow it everywhere. Their lives depend upon their being imprinted upon their mother, as she could not possibly follow all her goslings around at once, and they are not capable of looking after their own needs without her. In our own species, unlike most others, it is necessary instead for the mother to become imprinted on the baby because a human baby is too helpless to follow anyone or, indeed, to do anything towards maintaining contact with his mother besides signalling her if she fails to meet his expectations.

This all-important imprinting impulse is so strongly ingrained in the human mother that it takes precedence over all other considerations she may have; no matter how tired, no matter how hungry, thirsty or otherwise motivated by normal self-interest, she overridingly desires to feed and comfort this not very pretty total stranger. If it were not so, we would not have survived all these hundreds of thousands of generations. The imprinting, or bonding, geared into the sequence of hormonally triggered events at birth, must take place right away or it would be too late; a pre-historic mother could not have afforded to remain indifferent to a newborn baby even for a few minutes, so the powerful urge must be immediate. The provision for this in the continuum of events is an essential prerequisite to the smooth succession of stimuli and responses that follows as mother and baby begin their life together.

If the imprinting is prevented from taking place, if the baby is taken away when the mother is keyed to caress it, to bring it to her breast, into her arms and into her heart, or if the mother is too drugged to experience the bonding fully, what happens? It appears that the stimulus to imprint, if not responded to by the expected meeting with the baby, gives way to a state of grief. In the formative aeons of human births, when there was no object for the mother's surge of tenderness it was because the baby was stillborn. The psycho-biological response was one of mourning. When the moment is missed, the stimulus left without a response, the assumption of the continuum forces is that there is no baby and the imprinting urge must be annulled.

When, then, a modern hospital suddenly produces a baby hours, or even minutes, after the mother has gone into a physiological state of mourning, the result is often that she feels guilty about not being able to 'turn on mothering', or to 'love the baby very much' (see page 124), as well as suffering the classic civilized tragedy called normal postpartum depression . . . just when nature had her exquisitely primed for one of the deepest and most influential emotional events of her life.

A she-wolf true to the wolf continuum would be a more accurate mother to a human baby at this stage than the baby's biological mother in a bed one foot away. The wolf mother would be tangible; the human one could as well be on Mars.

In the maternity wards of Western civilization there is little chance of consolation from wolves. The newborn infant, with his skin crying out for the ancient touch of smooth, warmth-radiating, living flesh, is wrapped in dry, lifeless cloth. He is put in a box where he is left, no matter how he weeps, in a limbo that is utterly motionless (for the first time in all his body's experience, during the aeons of its evolution or during its eternity in the womb). The only sounds he can hear are the wails of other victims of the same ineffable agony. The sounds can mean nothing to him. He cries and cries; his lungs, new to air, are strained with the desperation in his heart. No one comes. Trusting in the rightness of life, as by nature he must, he does the only act he can, which is to cry on. Eventually, a timeless lifetime later, he falls asleep exhausted.

He awakes in a mindless terror of the silence, the motionlessness.

He screams. He is afire from head to foot with want, with desire, with intolerable impatience. He gasps for breath and screams until his head is filled and throbbing with the sound. He screams until his chest aches, until his throat is sore. He can bear the pain no more and his sobs weaken and subside. He listens. He opens and closes his fists. He rolls his head from side to side. Nothing helps. It is unbearable. He begins to cry again, but it is too much for his strained throat; he soon stops. He stiffens his desire-racked body, and there is a shadow of relief. He waves his hands and kicks his feet. He stops, able to suffer, unable to think, unable to hope. He listens. Then he falls asleep again.

When he awakens he wets his nappy and is distracted from his torment by the event. But the pleasant feeling of wetting and the warm, damp, flowing sensation around his lower body are quickly gone. The warmth is now immobile and turning cold and clammy. He kicks his legs, stiffens his body, sobs. Desperate with longing, his lifeless surroundings wet and uncomfortable, he screams through his misery until it is stilled by lonely sleep.

Suddenly he is lifted; his expectations come forward for what is to be his. The wet nappy is taken away. Relief. Living hands touch his skin. His feet are lifted and a new, bone-dry, lifeless cloth is folded around his loins. In an instant it is as though the hands had never been there, nor the wet nappy. There is no conscious memory, no inkling of hope. He is in unbearable emptiness, timeless, motionless, silent, wanting, wanting. His continuum tries its emergency measures, but they are all meant for bridging short lapses in correct treatment or for summoning relief from someone (it is assumed) who will want to provide it. His continuum has no solution for this extremity. The situation is beyond its vast experience. The infant, after breathing air for only a few hours, has already reached a point of disorientation from his nature beyond the saving powers of the mighty continuum. His tenure in the womb was the best approximation he is ever likely to know of the state of well-being in which it is his innate expectation that he will spend his lifetime. His nature is predicated upon the assumption that his mother is behaving suitably and that their motivations and consequent actions will naturally serve one another.

Someone comes and lifts him deliciously through the air. He is in life. He is carried a bit too gingerly for his taste, but there is motion. Then he is in his place. All the agony he has undergone is non-existent. He rests in the enfolding arms, and though his skin is sending no message of relief from the cloth, no news of live flesh on his flesh, his hands and mouth are reporting normal. The positive pleasure of life, which is continuum-normal, is almost complete. The taste and texture of the breast are there; the warm milk is flowing into his eager mouth; there is a heartbeat, which should have been his link, his reassurance of continuity from the womb; moving forms are visible that spell life. The sound of the voice is right too. There are only the cloth and the smell (his mother uses cologne) that leave something missing. He sucks and, when he feels full and rosy, dozes off.

When he awakens he is in hell. No memory, no hope, no thought can bring the comfort of his visit to his mother into this bleak purgatory. Hours pass and days and nights. He screams, tires, sleeps. He wakes and wets his nappy. By now there is no pleasure in this act. No sooner is the pleasure of relief prompted by his innards than it is replaced, as the hot, acid urine touches his by now chafed body, by a searing crescendo of pain. He screams. His exhausted lungs must scream to override the fiery stinging. He screams until the pain and screaming use him up before he falls asleep.

At his not unusual hospital the busy nurses change all nappies on schedule, whether they are dry, wet or long wet, and send the infants home, chafed raw, to be healed by someone who has time for such things.

By the time he is taken to his mother's home (surely it cannot be called his) he is well versed in the character of life. On a pre-conscious plane that will qualify all his further impressions, as it is qualified by them, he knows life to be unspeakably lonely, unresponsive to his signals and full of pain.

But he has not given up. His vital forces will try for ever to reinstate their balances as long as there is life.

Home is essentially indistinguishable from the maternity ward except for the chafing. The infant's waking hours are passed in yearning, wanting and interminable waiting for rightness to replace the silent void. For a few minutes a day his longing is suspended, and his terrible skin-crawling need to be touched, to be held and moved about, is relieved. His mother is one who, after much thought, has decided to allow him access to her breast. She loves him with a tenderness she has never known before. At first, it is hard for her to put him down after feeding, especially because he cries so desperately when she does. But she is convinced that she must, for her mother has told her (and *she* must know) that if she gives in to him now, he will be spoiled and cause trouble later. She wants to do everything right; she feels for a moment that the little life she holds in her arms is more important than anything else on earth.

She sighs and puts him gently in his cot, which is decorated with yellow ducklings and matches his whole room. She has worked hard to furnish it with fluffy curtains, a rug in the shape of a giant panda, a white dresser, a bath and a changing table equipped with powder, oil, soap, shampoo and hairbrush, all made and packed in colours especially for babies. On the wall there are pictures of baby animals dressed as people. The chest of drawers is full of little vests, Baby-Gros, bootees, caps, mittens and nappies. There is a toy woolly lamb stood at a beguiling angle on top and a vase of flowers – which have been cut off from their roots, for his mother also 'loves' flowers.

She straightens baby's vest and covers him with an embroidered sheet and a blanket bearing his initials. She notes them with satisfaction. Nothing has been spared in perfecting the baby's room, though she and her young husband cannot yet afford all the furniture they have planned for the rest of the house. She bends to kiss the infant's silky cheek and moves towards the door as the first agonized shriek shakes his body.

Softly she closes the door. She has declared war upon him. Her will must prevail over his. Through the door she hears what sounds like someone being tortured. Her continuum sense recognizes it as such. Nature does not make clear signals that someone is being tortured unless it is the case. *It is precisely as serious as it sounds*.

She hesitates, her heart pulled towards him, but resists and goes on her way. He has just been changed and fed. She is sure he does not *really* need anything therefore, and she lets him weep until he is exhausted.

He awakens and cries again. His mother looks in at the door to ascertain that he is in place; softly, so as not to awaken in him any hope of attention, she shuts the door again. She hurries to the kitchen, where she is working, and leaves that door open so that she can hear the baby, in case 'anything happens to him'.

The infant's screams fade to quavering wails. As no response is forthcoming, the motive power of the signal loses itself in the confusion of barren emptiness where the relief ought, long since, to have arrived. He looks about. There is a wall beyond the bars of his cot. The light is dim. He cannot turn himself over. He sees only the bars, immobile, and the wall. He hears meaningless sounds in a distant world. There is no sound near him. He looks at the wall until his eyes close. When they open again, the bars and the wall are exactly as before, but the light is dimmer.

Between eternities looking at the bars and wall, there are other eternities that take in both sets of side bars and the distant ceiling. Far away, at one side, there are motionless shapes, always there.

There are times when there is movement and something covering his ears, dimming sound, and great piles of cloth on top of him. At these times he can see the white plastic corner inside a pram and sometimes, when he is turned face up, the sky, the inside of the hood and, occasionally, great blocks that stand at a distance and slide past him. There are distant treetops, nothing to do with him either, and sometimes people looking down at him and talking, to one another usually but sometimes to him.

They shake a rattling object at him more often than not, and he feels, as it is so near, that he is close to life and reaches out and flaps his arms in anticipation of finding himself in his place. When the rattle is touched to his hand, he grasps it and puts it to his mouth. It is wrong. He waves his hands and the rattle flies away. It is brought back by a person. He learns that to throw a thing away will bring a person. He wants this promising figure to come, so he throws the rattle or any object at hand as long as the trick works. When the object ceases to be returned to him, there is the empty sky and the inside of the pram hood.

When he cries in the pram, he is often rewarded with signs of life. The pram is jiggled by his mother, who has learned that this tends to keep him quiet. The aching want of motion, experience, all that his antecedents had in *their* first months, is slightly lessened by the jiggling, which, in its meagre way, gives him some experience rather than none. The voices nearby are unassociated with anything happening to him, so have little value as fulfilment for his expectations. Still, they give him more than the silence of his nursery. His continuum experience quotient is near zero; his main actual experience is of want.

His mother weighs him regularly, proud of his progress.

What usable experience there is takes place during his few minutes' daily allotment of time in arms, plus piecemeal scraps which are acceptable to his separate requirements and added towards their quotas. At a moment when the baby is on his caretaker's lap, a child may rush up shouting and add the thrill of having action around him while he is safe. There is the welcome hum of the motor car when he is buffeted pleasantly on his mother's lap as it stops and goes in traffic. There are dog barks and other sudden noises. Some can be accepted in a pram; others, without the in-arms safety zone, frighten him.

The things that are put within his reach are meant to approximate what he is missing. Tradition dictates that toys be consoling to a grief-stricken infant. But it does so somehow without acknowledging the grief.

First and foremost, there is the teddy bear or similar soft doll 'to sleep with'. It is meant to give the infant a sense of constant companionship. The eventual fierce attachment to them that is sometimes formed is viewed as a charming bit of juvenile whimsy rather than a manifestation of acute deprivation in a child reduced to clinging to an inanimate object in its hunger for a companion who will not desert him. Pram-jiggling and cradles that rock offer another approximation. But the motion is so poor and clumsy a substitute for that in arms that it does little to still the longings of the isolated infant. Besides being inadequate, it is also infrequent. There are also toys hung over cots and prams that rattle, clink or chime when the infant touches them. They are often brightly coloured objects on strings, which add something to look at besides walls. They do attract his attention. But they are changed at long intervals, if at all, and do not begin to supply the developmental need for a variety of visual and auditory experience.

In spite of their paucity, jiggling, rocking, rattling, clinking and coloured forms are not lost. The continuum, ever ready to have its expectations realized, accepts whatever portion or fraction of them it gets. Although they come in rare fits and starts and are not combined as a continuum infant's experience would be (with in-arms sights and sounds, motions, smells and tastes acting upon his expectant senses in a harmonious pattern as they did in our common ancestors), and although some experiences are repeated with relative frequency and others left out entirely, none of this prevents their adoption as suitable material. The smooth continuity of experience, horizontally and vertically in time, gives our senses the illusion of a single operation. But it can be seen that each component operates separately, so that any next requirement in a single line of development can be accepted and, if sufficiently supplied, can give way to the next requirement in that line. Details of behaviour that appear to be related as cause and effect can be shown to be independently motivated.

This can be seen more clearly perhaps in the fulfilling of behavioural needs in other animals whose expressions of those needs are not inhibited by a necessity to give a rational explanation for doing what they feel impelled to do.

A capuchin monkey I brought back from my first expedition made a practice of eating as much of her banana (peeled and delivered to her by me) as she cared for at that sitting, and then, with a great air of doing nothing in particular, wrapped the remainder in a paper napkin, looking about as though unaware of what her hands were doing. She would then circle the area, posing as a casual stroller, suddenly discover the mysterious package and, with a show of mounting excitement, rip the covering from the treasure inside. Lo and behold! A half-eaten banana! Gadzooks! But then the pantomime would flag. She had just lunched and could not bring herself to pounce upon the prize. She would then rewrap the worried banana in the torn bits of paper and begin her performance anew. She convinced me that her impulse, her need, to search for and open food containers, such as fruit skins and nut shells, was entirely separate from and independent of her impulse to eat. Eliminating the hunting and cracking from the sequence that nature had always required of her evolving forebears (and which would have satisfied her experiential expectations) had been intended kindly on my part. I thought I was 'saving her trouble'. But I did not then understand the continuum. She followed her strongest impulse first and ate the food. As that impulse diminished with satiety, the next strongest came to the fore. She wished to hunt. Conditions were not conducive to the hunt, as the banana was naked and visible. Her solution was to set the scene herself, then perform the hunt. She was not pretending her excitement at unwrapping time. I am quite sure her heart rate was increased, and she showed all the physiological indications of genuine anticipation, even though the supposed object of that anticipation, eating, had already been attained. Just as each component of continuum experience is at once cause, effect, and goal, the true object of the hunting behaviour was satisfaction of the need for the hunting experience itself.

The object of life is life; the object of well-being is to encourage the behaviour that produces the sense of well-being. Procreation is to create procreators. The circular effect, far from being disappointingly pointless, is the best (and only) of all possible effects. That it is our nature being wholly itself is what makes it 'good', for good is a relative term. Relative to human potential, it is the best of all possible alternatives.

Human examples of behaviours fulfilling their own requirements in a sequence that precludes their serving any other purpose are plentiful. More often than not they are continuum-experience requirements excluded from the original sequence by a cultural pattern, by order of the intellect, on such grounds as time-wasting, inefficiency or wickedness. We shall consider some of these expressions in depth later, but as an illustration closely parallel to that of the monkey there is the phenomenon of hunting for sport rather than for food. Leftover impulses towards manual labour are used up on golf courses, in basement workshops and in yacht basins by those who can afford them; less fortunate deprivees content themselves with gardening, do-it-yourself projects, model building and amateur cookery. For women, usually those deprived even of housekeeping, there is tapestry, embroidery, flower arrangement, tea ceremony and a host of menial volunteer jobs done for charities, in understaffed hospitals, cast-off-clothing shops or soup kitchens.

The infant, then, is storing up every bit of positive experience he has, no matter what its sequence or how fragmentary its character. He must, however, at the end of the accumulating process, contain the requisite minimum of any experience to use it as the basis

for the next contingent set of experiences. Without the prior experiential quota having been met, the next-step experiences may
occur a thousand times without contributing to the maturing of
the individual.

While taking in whatever scraps of experience he can, the in-
arms-deprived infant is also developing compensatory behaviour to
relieve his agony. He kicks as violently as he can to mitigate the
tingling craving of his skin; he waves his arms; he rolls his head from
side to side to blur his senses; he stiffens his body, arching his back
with all the tension he can muster, to stop feeling it. He discovers a
little comfort in his own thumb; it relieves some of the incessant
desire in his mouth. He seldom actually sucks it; he is fed enough to
satisfy his hunger and needs to suck his thumb only when he wants
a feeding before his schedule says he can have it. Usually he simply
holds his thumb in his mouth against its unbearable emptiness, the
eternal loneliness, against a feeling that the centre of everything is
somewhere else.

His mother consults her mother and is told that persistent story
about thumb-sucking having a malefic influence upon the position
of future teeth. Inspired by concern for his welfare, she seeks out
deterrents such as foul-tasting paint for all his fingers, and when, in
his driving need, he still sucks it off one thumb, she ties his wrists to
the bars of his cot. But she finds he has turned his trapped limbs so
often in his struggle to free them that the ties have twisted until they
have begun to interfere with the circulation of one hand and will
soon have the same effect on the other. The battle goes on until she
mentions the problem to her dentist. He assures her that her mother
is mistaken, and the infant is permitted his meagre solace.

Before long the baby is able to smile and gurgle when someone
comes close enough to be signalled. If he is not picked up but given
some recognizable attention, he smiles and squeals to elicit more. If
he is picked up, his smile's mission is accomplished and returns only
to encourage some new pleasing behaviour in his companion, such
as making sounds at him, tickling his tummy, bouncing him on a
knee or mock-pinching his nose.

Because he smiles encouragingly when she comes to him, his
mother is convinced that she is the appreciated mother of a happy
baby. The bitter ordeal that is all the rest of his waking life does not

create any negative feeling towards her; on the contrary, it makes him all the more desperate to be with her.

As the infant matures and his cognitive faculties awaken, he becomes aware of a difference in his mother's manner when she discovers his nappy needs changing. She makes a sound of a clearly rejecting sort. She turns her head to one side in a way that shows that she does not like cleaning and making him comfortable. Her hands move brusquely and with the very least possible contact. Her eyes are cold; she does not smile.

As awareness of this attitude sharpens, the infant's pleasure at nappy-changing time, at being attended, touched and having his chronic, mild case of nappy rash temporarily relieved, becomes mixed with a bewilderment that is the precursor of fear and guilt.

The fear of displeasing his mother grows with cognition, and her displeasure is occasioned by an increasing number of his actions, including pulling her hair, spilling his food, drooling on her clothes (and, mysteriously, on some clothes more than others), poking his fingers in her mouth, pulling her necklace, throwing his rattle or bear out of his pram or knocking over a teacup with an unaimed kick.

Most of these acts are difficult to connect with her reaction. He has not noticed the teacup falling; he does not understand what there is about pulling her necklace that suddenly makes her treat him as hateful; he is utterly unaware of drooling on anything; and he only dimly perceives that knocking over his porridge bowl, done to get attention, incurs the wrong sort. Still, he feels it is better than no attention and continues to knock it off the device in which he is now trapped to be given his food. When his mother tries to feed him with a spoon, he waves his arms and kicks and squeals in an attempt to turn it into a more satisfactory occasion. He wants the sense of rightness that is somewhere to be found in the ingredients: his mother's presence, his food and himself. But despite all his signals he cannot bring it about. Instead they turn what attention she is giving him into rejection of a kind that, in time, will become easier for him to interpret, unlike all the early eternities of neglect that he could not interpret at all. His neglectedness and his longing are already fundamental qualities of life. He has never known anything else. For him, Self is wanting, waiting; Other is withholding, unresponsive or opposing. These conditions, though they continue throughout his life, may go unnoticed for the simple reason that he cannot conceive of an alternative kind of relation of Self to Other.

The missing experiences of the in-arms phase, the consequent gap where his feeling of confidence ought to be and his ineffable state of alienation will condition and influence all that he becomes as he grows up around the rim of the abyss where a rich sense of self might have burgeoned. But it must be understood that there is no mechanism in his early life that can take account of an inadequate mother, a mother without a working continuum, one who does not respond to infant signals, one who is set against, not for, the fulfilment of his expectations. Later, as his intellect develops, he may 'understand' that her interests and his are at odds, and as he grows up he may struggle to behave independently to save himself. But at base he can never fully *believe* that his mother does not love him unconditionally, simply because he exists, though he may shout from the housetops that he *knows* better. All the evidence to the contrary, all his intellectual comprehension of the facts, all his protestations and renunciations of her and acts of rebellion against her based upon these evidences of her inimical position to him – none can free him from his fundamental assumption that she loves him, that she must love him, somehow, in spite of everything. 'Hatred' for a mother (or mother figure) is the expression of a losing battle to free oneself of that assumption.

The growth of independence and the power to mature emotionally spring largely from the in-arms relationship in all its aspects. One cannot therefore become independent of one's mother except *through* her, through her playing her correct role, giving the in-arms experience and allowing one to graduate from it upon fulfilment.

But one can never free oneself of a non-continuum mother. Need for her cannot but continue. One can only struggle on the hook, like the 'atheist' who shakes his fist at God's throne in the heavens shouting, 'I do not believe in you!' and blasphemies that are worth uttering only because they take His name in vain.

Dr John Bowlby, of London's Tavistock Clinic, was commissioned by the World Health Organization to make a report on the fate of 'children homeless in their native countries', with regard to their state of mental health.* His subjects were the most extreme cases of maternal deprivation in each country and numbered in the thousands. The information he collected from workers in the field covered many years and situations: children in institutions from infancy, some in foster homes, others neglected by their own parents; babies and children in hospitals for critical months or years in their early development; wartime evacuees; and victims of every sort of circumstance that kept them from even that exiguous degree of maternal contact known as normal.

Causes other than 'emotional deprivation resulting from lack of mothering' were eliminated in the study only after scrupulous examination of the evidence. The picture painted by the descriptions and statistics in the report is one of horrendous personal agonies, multiplied beyond the power of the mind to conceive, and chronicles the empty lives that follow the deprivations, the 'affectionless characters' of the most grossly deprived, those who have lost the ability to form attachments, which is to say, to know the value of life itself, ever. It documents the torments of those still active in the battle for their birthright measure of love, lying, stealing, attacking brutally or clinging with the intensity of leeches to mother figures, regressing to infantile behaviour in the hope of being treated at last as the infant that is still within them starving for its experience. It records the perpetuation of these desperate people as they produce children they cannot love, who grow up like themselves, anti-self, antisocial, incapable of giving, destined forever to go hungry.

They are the spelled-out, indisputable evidence, examples, proofs, for anyone who can doubt it, of the quintessential primacy of infant experience to the human personality. The extreme nature of their cases is but a magnifying glass through which one can see more clearly the deprivations and effects of the broader, more various and subtle range comprising normality. These 'normal' deprivations are by now so tangled in the meshes of our cultures that they are almost entirely unremarked *except* at such extremes as manifest themselves in cost and danger to the rest of us (through violence, insanity and crime, for example), and even then they are regarded without comprehension of any but the dimmest sort.

* J. Bowlby, *Maternal Care and Mental Health*, W.H.O., 1951.

Since the intellect, with its parade of theories, took charge of their treatment, the vicissitudes of human infants have been many and terrible. Reasons for modifying or revolutionizing their care have never had much resemblance to continuum 'reasons', and when they *have* been in the correct direction, but without relationship to continuum principle, they have been fragmentary and infertile.

One such bit of theory was implemented in an American maternity ward, where it occurred to someone to pipe a heartbeat over a loudspeaker to infants in their first agonies of experiential deprivation. The effect of this small contribution was so calming and resulted in such improvement in the infants' health that the experiment received world-wide attention.

Another, similar but independent, experiment was done by a specialist in premature infant care. It showed notable improvement in development in the tiny subjects when the incubators were kept in motion by a machine. In both situations the infants gained weight faster and cried less.

Harry Harlow made spectacular experiments proving the importance of cuddliness in mother monkeys to the psychological development of infant monkeys.*

Jane Van Lawick-Goodall, in what must surely be one of the greatest ironies of all time, found more inspiring examples of infant care in her chimpanzee friends, whose behaviour, even as another species, is closer to that of the human continuum than the behaviour of present-day humans. Speaking of the application of their example to her own child, she writes, 'He was not left to scream in his cot. Wherever we went we took him with us so that though his environment was often changing, his relationship with his parents remained stable.'† She further reports that at four, her son is 'obedient, extremely alert and lively, mixes well with other children and adults alike, is relatively fearless and is thoughtful of others'. But perhaps her most significant statement is this: 'In addition, and quite contrary to the predictions of many of our friends, he is very independent.' Yet, again, unconscious of the underlying principles,

* H. F. Harlow, 'The Development of Affectioned Patterns in Infant Monkeys', in Brian M. Foss (ed.), *Determinants of Infant Behaviour*, London, 1961.
† J. Van Lawick-Goodall, *In the Shadow of Man*, Boston, 1971.

she isolates her fragment of truth from further insight with her next sentence: 'But then, of course, he might have been like this anyway, even if we had brought him up in a quite different way.'

Illuminating research might be done on the influence of Queen Victoria's acceptance of the pram (bringing it into common use) upon the character of the subsequent generation and the effect on Western family life. Would that the invention of the pram had met the same fate as the playpen I saw invented one day in a Yequana village.

It was nearly finished when I noticed Tududu working on it. It had upright sticks lashed with vines to an upper and a lower square frame, like a strip-cartoon version of a prehistoric playpen. It had cost a good deal of labour, and Tududu looked quite pleased with himself when he lopped off the last protuberant stick end. He cast about for Cananasinyuwana, his son, who had taken his first step about a week earlier. No sooner had Tududu sighted the tot than he snatched him up and put him triumphantly in the new invention. Cananasinyuwana stood uncomprehending for a few seconds at the centre, then made a move to one side, turned about and realized that he was trapped. In an instant he was screaming a message of utter horror, a sound rarely heard from children of his society. It was unequivocal. The playpen was wrong, unsuitable for human babies. Tududu's continuum sense, as strong as any Yequana's, did not hesitate in interpreting the shrieks of his son. He pulled him out and let him run away to throw himself upon his mother for the minutes he needed to counteract the shock before he was ready to go out again to play. Tududu accepted the failure of his experiment without question; after a moment's last look at his handiwork, he smashed the playpen to bits with an axe, and as the wood he had used was green, he did not gain so much as a pile of firewood from his morning's efforts. I have no doubt that it was neither the first nor the last such invention by a Yequana, but their continuum sense would never permit so patent an error to last long. If our continuum sense had not been so elemental a force in human behaviour for our two million years of stability, it would not have been able to contain the dangers inherent in our highly developed intellect. That it has lately been disempowered to the point where instability, or 'progress', appears to us to be our ever more glorious destiny does not alter one jot the fact that the continuum sense is intrinsic to our very humanness. Tududu smashing the playpen is what we are evolved to be, what we would have continued to be had our sense remained unclouded, unbetrayed by whatever derailed it, leaving us so much in the dangerously ignorant hands of the intellect.

4: Growing Up

When all the shelter and stimulus of his experience in arms have been given in full measure, the baby can look forward, outward, to the world beyond his mother, sure of himself and accustomed to a well-being that his nature tends to maintain. He is expectant of the next set of appropriate experiences. He begins crawling, returning often to assure himself of his mother's availability. Finding her constant, he ventures further afield and returns less frequently, as crawling (on elbows, inner legs, and belly) gives way to creeping (hands and knees) and his increasing agility keeps pace with his curiosity about the surrounding terrain, as the continuum provides.

The need for physical contact tapers off quickly when its experience quota has been filled, and a baby, tot, child or adult will require the reinforcement it gives him only in moments of stress with which his current powers cannot cope. These moments become increasingly rare, and self-reliance grows with a speed, depth and breadth that would seem prodigious to anyone who has known only civilized children deprived of the complete in-arms experience. In children who have some lines of development going ahead, while others hang back waiting for completion, the effect is to divide their motives: they may never be able to want anything without also wanting to be the centre of attention, never be able to devote their minds singly to the problem before them when part of them still craves the mindless euphoria of an infant in the arms of someone who solves all problems. They cannot wholly apply themselves to the use of their growing strength and skill while part of them longs to be helpless in arms. Every effort is in conflict to some extent with an underlying desire for the effortless success of the beloved babe.

The child with a solid background of continuum experience resorts to physical comforting from his mother only in emergencies. One Yequana boy I knew came to me clinging to his mother and screaming at the top of his lungs from a toothache. He was about ten years old and so unfailingly self-reliant and helpful that I had supposed him to be highly disciplined. To my civilized view, he seemed a master of keeping his feelings to himself, and I therefore expected that in the present situation he would be making a terrific effort not to cry or to let his companions see him in such a state. But it was clear that he was making no attempt to suppress his reaction to the pain or his need for the primordial comfort of his mother's arms.

No one fussed, but everyone understood. A few of his playmates stood by to watch me extract the tooth. They did not have any difficulty in accepting his sudden departure from their gallant ranks into infantile dependence upon his mother; there was no hint of mockery from them, none of shame from him. His mother was there, passively available, while he submitted to the extraction. He flinched and shrieked even louder several times when I touched the tooth, but he never pulled away or looked angry at me for causing the pain. When at last I worked the tooth free of the gum and stopped the hole with gauze, he was white in the face and went to his hammock exhausted. In less than an hour he reappeared alone, the colour back in his cheeks and his equanimity restored. He said nothing but smiled and poked about nearby for a few minutes to show me he was well, then wandered off to join the other boys.

Another time it was a man of about twenty: I was doing my best to excise the beginnings of gangrene from his toe. The pain must have been excruciating. While offering no resistance to my clearing the wound with a hunting knife, he wept without any sign of restraint on his wife's lap. She, like the little boy's mother, was completely relaxed, not putting herself in her husband's place at all but serenely accessible, as he buried his face in her body when the pain was greatest or rolled his head from side to side on her lap as he sobbed. The eventual presence of about half the village at the scene did not appear to affect any effort towards either self-control or dramatization.

Since Yequana women usually live with their mothers as long as the latter are alive, and the husbands leave their mothers and take a place in the wife's family, it is fairly common to find the wife taking the maternal position towards her husband in his crises. The wife has her own mother to draw upon but instinctively gives maternal support to her man when *he* needs it. For orphaned adults too there is a custom that provides for adoption into another family. The strain on that family's resources is minimal, as the adult Yequana contributes more than he consumes in his or her family and receives from them a tacit guarantee of support if and when it is needed. That assurance alone, even if it is never called upon, is a stabilizing factor. The requirement for emotional insurance is an accepted part of human nature among the Yequana, one that it is in the interest of society to honour. It is another safeguard against any of its members becoming antisocialized by the pressure that circumstance might bring to bear upon his natural sociality. This respect for every individual's continuum requirements is surely the most effective kind of crime prevention.

With the commencement of crawling, the baby begins to cash in the powers accumulated passively through his previous experience combined with the physiological development that renders the powers usable. In general, his first expeditions are short and cautious and there is almost no need for his mother or caretaker to take a hand in his activities. Like all little animals, he has a keen talent for self-preservation and a realistic sense of his capabilities. If his mother suggests to his social instincts that he is expected to leave his safe conduct to her, he will cooperatively do so. If he is constantly watched and steered into moving where his mother thinks he ought to go, stopped and run after when self-motivated, he soon learns to stop being responsible for himself as she shows him what she expects.

One of the deepest impulses in the very social human animal is to do what he perceives is expected of him. (This is not at all the same as doing what he is told.) His incipient intellectual abilities are slight, but his instinctive tendencies are as strong at the first as at the last moment of his life. The combination of these two powers, the reasoning one, dependent on learning, and the instinctive one, finely versed in the same sort of innate knowledge that guides other animals through their entire lives – the result of their interplay – is the human character and the uniquely human potential for intellectually refined, instinctive efficiency.

Besides his tendencies towards experiment and caution, the baby has, as ever, expectations. He expects the range his ancestors enjoyed. He expects not only space and the freedom to move in it but a variety of encounters as well. He is more flexible now in what he expects. The strict requirements of earliest experience have gradually broadened during the in-arms phase and, at the crawling and creeping phases, more and more become expectations of *kinds* of experience rather than of precise circumstance and treatment.

But there are still margins within which the baby's experience must fall if they are to serve him. He cannot develop properly without the type and variety of opportunity and the kind of participation from others that he requires. The objects, situations and people available must be more than he can use, so that he can discover and enlarge his capabilities among them; and, of course, they must change to a suitable degree, suitably often, but not *too* radically or *too* often. Suitability is, as always, dictated by precedent, by the character of our evolving ancestors' experience during their baby-hoods.

In a Yequana village, for example, there are curiosities, hazards and associations of more than adequate quantity and quality for a creeping baby. When his first forays are made, he is testing everything. He is measuring his own strength and agility, and he is testing all he meets, forming concepts and making distinctions in time, space and form. He is also creating a new relationship with his mother, which moves slowly from direct dependence upon her to knowledge of her dependability, and counts on her for support in ever less frequent times of need.

Among the Yequana the attitude of the mother or caretaker of a baby is relaxed, attentive to some other occupation than baby-minding but receptive at all times to a visit from the crawling or creeping adventurer. She does not stop her cooking or other work unless her full attention is actually required. She does not throw her arms open to the little seeker for reassurance but, in her calm way, allows him the freedom of her person, or an arm-supported ride on her hip if she is moving about.

She does not initiate the contacts nor contribute to them except in a passive way. It is the baby who seeks her out and shows her by his behaviour what he wants. She complies fully and willingly but does not add anything more. He is the active, she the passive agent in all their dealings; he comes to her to sleep when he is tired, to be fed when he is hungry. His explorations of the wide world are counterpointed and reinforced by his resort to her and by his sense of her constancy while he is away.

He neither demands nor receives her full attention, for he has no store of longings, no ancient hungers, to gnaw at his devotion to the here and now. Consistent with the economical character of nature, he wants no more than he needs.

When he goes about on hands and knees, a baby can travel at a fair speed. Among the Yequana, I watched uneasily as one creeper rushed up and stopped at the edge of a pit five feet deep that had been dug for mud to make walls. In his progress about the compound, he did this several times a day. With the inattentiveness of an animal grazing at the edge of a cliff, he would tumble to a sitting position, as often as not facing away from the pit. Occupied with a stick or stone or his fingers or toes, he played and rolled about in every direction, seemingly heedless of the pit, until one realized he landed everywhere but in the danger zone. The non-intellect-directed mechanisms of self-preservation worked unfailingly and, being so precise in their calculations, functioned equally well at any distance from the pit, starting from the very edge. Unattended or, more often, at the periphery of attention of a group of children playing with the same lack of respect for the pit, he took charge of his own relationships with all the surrounding possibilities. The only suggestion from the members of his family and society was that they expected him to be able to look after himself. Though he still could not walk, he knew where comfort could be found if he wanted it – but he seldom did. If his mother went to the river or the distant garden, she often took him along, lifting him to her by his forearm and counting on his help to balance himself on her hip or hold on to the sling if she wore one to support his weight. Wherever she went, if she put him down in a safe place, she expected him to remain safe without supervision.

A baby has no suicidal inclinations and a full set of survival mechanisms, from the senses, on the grossest level, to what looks like very serviceable everyday telepathy on the less accountable levels. He behaves like any little animal that cannot call upon experience to serve its judgement; he does the safe thing, unaware of making a choice. He is naturally protective of his own well-being, expected to be so by his people and enabled to be so by his inborn abilities plus his stage of development and experience. But the latter is so meagre at this age of six, eight or ten months that it can contribute little in any case and next to nothing in new situations. It is instinct that provides for his self-preservation. Still, he is no longer only a mammal turned primate; he begins to take on specifically human characteristics. He tends more every day towards learning his people's culture. He begins at this time to distinguish between his father's and his mother's roles in his life. His mother's remains steadfastly what all people's roles have been until now: that of a giver and caretaker who expects nothing in return but the satisfaction of having given. His mother cares for him simply because he is there; his existence is reason enough to guarantee her love. Her unconditional acceptance remains constant as his father emerges as an important figure interested in his developing social behaviour and his advance towards independence. The father's constant love maintains the same character as the mother's but has an overlay of approval contingent upon the performance of the child. Thus nature ensures both stability and incentive towards sociality. Later the father will distinguish himself more and more clearly as the representative of society and will guide the child, showing by example what is expected, towards choices of behaviour appropriate to the particular customs in which he will participate.

Brothers, sisters and other people all begin to take on differentiated places in his world. For some time to come there will be an element of the maternal, albeit a diminishing one, in all his associates. He will need to be deferred to and protected while he grows in self-reliance. He will continue to signal according to his needs, and the cues will continue to be irresistible to his elders until they fade away with his adolescence. In the meantime, *he* will become susceptible to the tenderness cues in younger children and behave towards them in the maternal way while giving off similar sparks to the more developed children and adults upon whom he still depends for a measure of *his* life-support system.

For boys, men will become the major inspiration and example in learning their part in the culture, as that is how things are done in their society. Little girls will imitate women when their stage of development dictates that association should change to participation.

The tools will be provided if they are difficult to manufacture. For instance, it is within the capability of a child to paddle a canoe, or play at it, long before he can carve a paddle for himself. When the time comes, he or she is given a scaled-down paddle made by an adult. Before they can talk, boys are provided with little bows and arrows that give valuable practice, as the arrows are straight and accurately reflect their skill.

I was present at the first moments of one little girl's working life. She was about two years old. I had seen her with the women and girls, playing as they grated manioc into a trough. Now she was taking a piece of manioc from the pile and rubbing it against the grater of a girl near her. The chunk was too big; she dropped it several times trying to draw it across the rough board. An affectionate smile and a smaller piece of manioc came from her neighbour, and her mother, ready for the inevitable impulse to show itself, handed her a tiny grating board of her own. The little girl had seen the women grating as long as she could remember and immediately rubbed the nubbin up and down her board like the others.

She lost interest in less than a minute and ran off, leaving her little grater in the trough and no noticeable inroads on the manioc. No one made her feel her gesture was funny or a 'surprise'; the women did, indeed, expect it sooner or later, as they are all familiar with the fact that children do join in the culture, though their approach and pace are dictated by forces within themselves. That the end result will be social, cooperative and entirely voluntary is not in question. Adults and older children contribute only the help and supplies that the child cannot possibly provide for himself. A pre-talking child is perfectly able to make his needs clear, and there is no point in offering anything he does not require; *the object of a child's activities, after all, is the development of self-reliance. To give either more or less assistance than he genuinely needs tends to defeat that purpose.*

Caretaking, like assistance, is by request only. Feeding to nourish the body and cuddling to nourish the soul are neither proffered nor withheld but are always available, simply and gracefully, as a matter of course. Above all, the child is respected as a good thing in all respects. There is no concept of a 'bad child', nor, conversely, any distinction made about 'good children'. It is assumed that the child is social, not antisocial, in his motives. What he does is accepted as the act of an innately 'right' creature. This assumption of rightness, or sociality, as an inbuilt characteristic of human nature is the essence of the Yequana attitude towards others, of any age. It is also the keystone upon which the child's development is abetted by his associates, parental or other.

To educate, in its original sense, is to 'lead out', but although this may have some advantage over the more widespread interpretation, to 'hammer in', neither way is consistent with the child's evolved expectations. Being led out, or guided, by an elder is tantamount to interference with the child's development, since it leads him away from his natural, most efficient path to one less so. *The assumption of innate sociality* is at direct odds with the fairly universal civilized belief that a child's impulses need to be curbed in order to make him social. There are those who believe that reasoning and pleading for 'cooperativeness' with the child will accomplish this curbing better than threat or mental or physical insult. But the assumption that every child has an antisocial nature, in need of manipulation to become socially acceptable, is germane to both these points of view as well as to all the more common ones between the two extremes. If there is anything fundamentally foreign to *us* in continuum societies like the Yequana, it is this assumption of innate sociality. It is by starting from this assumption and its implications that the seemingly unbridgeable gap between their strange behaviour, with resultant high well-being, and our careful calculations, with an enormously lower degree of well-being, becomes intelligible.

As we have seen, either more or less assistance than a child demands is detrimental to his progress. Outside initiatives, therefore, or unsolicited guidance, are of no positive use to him. He can make no more progress than his own motivations encompass. *A child's curiosity and desire to do things himself are the definition of his capacity to learn without sacrificing any part of his whole development. Guidance can only heighten certain abilities at the expense of others, but nothing can heighten the full spectrum of his capabilities beyond its in-built limits.* The price a child pays for being guided into what his parents think best for him (or themselves) is the diminution of his wholeness. His total well-being, the reflection of all his aspects nourished or starved, is directly affected. His elders do a great deal to determine his own choices of behaviour by their example and by what he perceives to be their expectations, but they cannot add anything to his wholeness by substituting their motives for his own, or 'telling him what to do'.

Ideally, giving the child an example, or lead, to follow is not done expressly to influence him but means doing what one has to do normally: not giving special attention to the child but creating the atmosphere of minding one's own business by way of priority, noticing the child only when he requires it and then no more than is useful. A child with a full complement of in-arms experience will have no need to beg attention in excess of his physical requirements, for he will not, like the children one has known in civilized circumstances, need reassurance to affirm either his existence or his lovableness.

Applying the principle in the easiest situation, a civilized mother would go about her domestic work with a little girl taking whatever interest she takes but allowed to sweep with a small broom when she is inspired to do so or dust or vacuum (if she can manage the model of cleaner in her home) or help wash dishes standing on a chair. The breakage will be inconsiderable and the little girl will not fall off the chair, unless her mother is so clear in her expectation of disaster that the child's social impulse (to do what she understands is expected of her) drives her to comply. An anxious look, a word of what is in the mother's mind ('Don't drop that!') or a promise ('Mind! You'll fall!'), although working in opposition to the child's self-preservation and imitative tendencies, can, if one persists, eventually cause her to obey, drop the plate, and/or fall off the chair.

Among the uniquenesses of man as a species is his intellect's ability to contradict his evolved nature. Once the continuum has been derailed, its stabilizers overbalanced to a point of impotence, aberrations appear thick and fast, as the intellect is almost as likely to do harm as good in its uninformed, well-intentioned, one-thing-at-a-time considerations of the incalculable mass of factors relevant to any behaviour.

One of the oddest outcomes of loss of faith in the continuum is the ability of adults to make children run away from them. Nothing could be closer to the continuum heart of a baby than to stay close to his mother in unfamiliar territory. All our mammal relatives, and birds, reptiles and fish as well, are followed by their young, in whose clear interest it is to do so. A Yequana tot would not dream of straying from his mother on a forest trail, for she does not look behind to see *whether* he is following; she does not suggest that there is a choice to be made or that it is *her* job to keep them together; she only slows her pace to one he can maintain. Knowing this, the babe will cry out if he cannot keep up for one reason or another. A minor fall from which he can pick himself up and run a little to make up the lost seconds seldom rates even that call. Her manner shows him that she is both businesslike and patient if ever she does have to wait for him. It suggests that she knows that he will not take any more time than is gracefully necessary before they can continue together on their way. There is nothing of the judge in her. Her assumption of his innate sociality works with his tendency to do what he perceives she expects. Stopping or going, that basic assumption remains unchanged and unquestioned.

Yet, in spite of the millions of years of precedent and the consistent examples of our fellow animals and still quite a few of our fellow men, we have managed to persuade our tots to run away.

After the fourth expedition I was struck by the number of small children being chased by grown-ups in Manhattan's Central Park. Mothers and nannies were to be seen flapping about, bent unbecomingly at the hips, hands outstretched and voices shrill, begging with unconvincing threats for the fugitive toddlers to come to heel. They varied that nerve-racking performance with attempts to carry on park-bench conversations with one another while calling out to charges who were nearing the limits of their allowed distances; or the women leapt up and rushed after outright escapees who had caught on to the rules of the game and taken the first relaxation of surveillance as the signal for a break.

A simple suggestion like 'Don't go where I can't see you!' said with a note of apprehension (expectation) causes much traffic in lost-child departments and, when mixed with a 'Watch out, you'll hurt yourself!' promise, a good number of drownings, serious falls and road accidents as well. Mindful predominantly of playing the part expected of him in his battle of wills with his caretaker, the little challenger is out of responsible balance with his surroundings, and his self-preservation system is handicapped. He is thus reduced, quite unconsciously, to following the absurd order to hurt himself. If he awakens in hospital, he will not, however, be very surprised to learn that he has been hit by a car, as his VIP caretaker has so often promised him he would be.

The unconscious mind does not reason. Its mechanism for making habit of experience, for automating recurrent behaviour in order to release the conscious mind, for stabilizing and maintaining, for cataloguing and cross-referencing data, is one that is too demanding for a faculty as unreliable as reason, which is its very antithesis. It is too observant to be persuaded that something is what someone says it is when her tone and actions belie it. Therefore a child may very well understand the reasoning of the caretaker and even reason similarly, while being motivated to behave contrarily. In other words, he is more likely to do what he *senses is expected of him* than what he is asked to do. His chronic, unsatisfied longing for acceptance by his mother can reinforce to the point of self-destructiveness his need to do what he feels is expected by her or her representatives. A sound, continuum child will have a working set of innate tendencies to do the suitable thing, like imitating, exploring, examining, not injuring himself or other people, coming in out of the rain, making pleasing noises and faces when people behave correctly, responding to signals in younger children and so on; a deprived child or one who is expected to behave antisocially can transgress *his* innate sense of fitness to the extent that his requirements and susceptibility to the expectations of others have been transgressed.

The familiar expedients of praise and blame wreak havoc upon the motives of children, especially the smallest ones. If the child does something useful, like putting on his own clothes or feeding the dog, bringing in a handful of field flowers or making an ashtray from a lump of clay, nothing can be more discouraging than an expression of surprise that he has behaved socially. 'Oh, what a good girl!' 'Look what Georgie has made all by himself!' and similar exclamations imply that sociality is unexpected, uncharacteristic and unusual in the child. His reason may be pleased, but his feeling will be of uneasiness at having failed to do what was expected, that which makes him most truly part of his culture, tribe and family. Even among children themselves, a phrase like 'Gosh, look what Mary made at school!', said with sufficient wonder, will make Mary feel uncomfortably removed from her playmates, as though they had said in the same tone, 'Gosh, Mary's fat!' or thin or tall or short or clever or stupid but somehow not as she was expected to be. Blame, especially if it is reinforced with a 'You *always* do that' label, is also destructive, with its suggestion that antisocial behaviour is expected. 'Just like you to lose your handkerchief', 'He's full of mischief', a hopeless shrug, a blanket indictment like 'Boys will be boys', implying that the badness is solidly built in, or a simple facial expression demonstrating that a misbehaviour was *no* surprise, work with the same disastrous effect as surprise or praise for social behaviour.

Creativeness can also be scotched by the use of the child's need to cooperate. One merely says something like 'Take your paints out into the garden; I don't want you making a mess in here.' The message that the painting will be a mess will not be lost, and the creative urge would have to be tremendous to overcome the child's quintessential need to do what his mother expects. Said with a sweet smile or shouted like a war cry, the bad-child pronouncement is equally effective.

The assumption of innate sociality requires some knowledge of the content as well as the form of the child's tendencies and expectations. It is clear that they are imitative, cooperative and inclined to preserve the individual and the species, but they also include such specifics as knowing how to care for infants and having the ability to do so. To give the profound maternal urge in little girls no quarter, to channel it away to dolls when there are real infants about, is among other things a serious disservice to the children of the little girl when she grows up. Even before she can understand instructions from her own mother, a little girl, given the opportunity, behaves instinctively towards infants in the precise manner required by infants since time immemorial. By the time she is old enough to consider alternative methods, she is already a long-standing expert in baby care and does not feel there is any advantage in thinking about it. She goes on throughout her childhood taking care of babies whenever she can, in her own family or among her neighbours, and, by the time she marries, not only has nothing to discuss with the Dr Spocks but also has two strong carrying arms and a repertoire of positions and movements with which babies can be held while cooking, gardening, cleaning, paddling canoes, grooming, sleeping, dancing, bathing, eating or anything else. She also has a deeply ingrained sense that would rebel against any action unsuitable to her continuum or that of a baby.

I saw little Yequana girls from the age of three or four (sometimes they looked even younger) taking full charge of infants. It was clearly their favourite occupation but did not prevent their doing other things at the same time – tending fires, fetching water and so on. They did not tire of their charges as they would have of dolls. The continuum is at its strongest, it seems, in the protection of infants, and the endless patience and loving care they need is there in every child, boys included. Though boys are seldom given long-time care of infants, they are very fond of picking them up and playing with them. Young men in their teens look for infants to play with when they come back from their day's activities. They throw the babies high in the air and catch them, laughing loudly and sharing a hilarious time with their tiny tribesmen, whose range of experience and sense of lovableness is happily enriched.

Perhaps as essential as the assumption of innate sociality in children and adults is a respect for each individual as his own proprietor. The notion of ownership of other persons is absent among the Yequana. The idea that this is 'my child' or 'your child' does not exist. Deciding what another person should do, no matter what his age, is outside the Yequana vocabulary of behaviours. There is great interest in what everyone does but no impulse to persuade – let alone coerce – anyone. A child's will is his motive force. There is no slavery – for how else can one describe imposing one's will on another and coercion by threat or punishment? The Yequana do not feel that a child's inferior strength and dependence upon them imply that they should treat him or her with less respect than an adult. No orders are given to a child that run counter to his own inclinations as to how to play, how much to eat, when to sleep and so on. But where his help is required, he is expected to comply instantly. Commands like 'Bring some water!' 'Chop some wood!' 'Hand me that!' or 'Give the baby a banana!' are given with the same assumption of innate sociality, in the firm knowledge that a child wants to be of service and to join in the work of his people. No one watches to see whether the child obeys – there is no doubt of his will to cooperate. As the social animal he is, he does as he is expected without hesitation and to the very best of his ability.

It works incredibly well. But during my second expedition I noticed a boy about one year old who seemed to have strayed from the centre of his continuum in some way. I cannot say what caused it, but it may not be a coincidence that his father, an old fellow called Wenito, was the only Yequana in the area who spoke Spanish, having worked in the rubber boom during his youth, and his wife knew some of the Pemontong language, showing she had lived among the Indians farther east. They may, in their unusually cosmopolitan lives, have picked up some usage on such impressive authority that their own continua were encroached upon. I do not know. But Wididi, their son, was the only child I ever saw having a tantrum, shrieking at the top of his lungs in protest at something rather than crying in the unstrained way one heard when any other baby happened to cry. Sometimes, after he started walking, he hit other children. Interestingly, the other children regarded him without emotion; the idea of aggressiveness was so foreign to them that they took it as though they had been struck by a tree branch or from some other natural cause; they never dreamt of striking back and went on with their games without even excluding Wididi. I saw him again when he was about five. His father had died, and Anchu, the village chief, who had been Wenito's close friend, was taking on the role of father, or leader, for Wididi. The boy was still far astray from the happy Yequana norm. There was a certain tension in his face and in the way he moved his body, which was reminiscent of a civilized child.

On our journey to the airstrip that we had cleared by the Canaracuni River, Anchu brought Wididi, as the other members of our crew brought their little boys along for the experience. Wididi was already well versed in canoeing, and as the heaviest work is done at the bow and the subtle manoeuvring at the stern, he often paddled stern while the chief did the work in front. Few words passed between them, but Anchu's quiet, constant expectation of rightness was almost palpable. On the way, when we handed round pieces of meat, Anchu always shared his with Wididi. It sometimes appeared that the boy had become as serene and efficient as other Yequana boys.

But one day, in the camp beside the airstrip, Anchu was preparing to go hunting, and Wididi watched him with mounting apprehension. His face reflected dreadful conflict, and his lips began to quiver as he followed the man's every move with his eyes. When Anchu's bow and arrows were ready the boy's chest was shaking with spasms and then sobs. Anchu had said nothing, nor had he given any sort of look of judgement upon him, but Wididi knew that boys went out hunting with their leaders and he did not want to go. There was no one to argue with but himself, for Anchu was simply going hunting, and what Wididi did was up to Wididi. His antisocial side said no; his innate sociality, now in the process of being liberated by Anchu, said yes. Anchu took the bow and arrows and started up the path. Wididi's whole body shook as he screamed. By now his motive and countermotive were evenly matched and he simply stood and howled, racked by indecision. I understood nothing then of the principles at work. I only saw the boy in torment because he had not gone with Anchu. I went to him and, putting my hands on his shoulders, hurried him along the path. I ran with him out to the savanna, where Anchu was just disappearing into the jungle at one side. I called to him to wait, but Anchu neither turned round nor slowed his pace. I called again, louder, but he disappeared into the forest. I pushed Wididi ahead and bade him hurry. I thought I was helping Wididi and preventing Anchu from being disappointed, but of course I was interfering, and with the clumsiness typical of my culture, I was substituting my will for the child's, trying to make him *do* the right thing, while Anchu had been working on the far sounder principle of freeing him to *want* to do the right thing. My contribution may have set Wididi's progress back by weeks. Anchu's system may have been on the verge of throwing the balance by removing all pressure from Wididi so his natural urge to be part of things could overcome whatever had caused him to rebel.

I found the complete absence of pressure by persuasion, by the imposition of one individual's will upon another, difficult to believe or understand, despite the Yequana's perseverance in showing me examples of it.

At the beginning of the third expedition, while we were preparing to go upriver, I asked Anchu if Tadehah, a boy of about nine or ten, might come with us. We were filming and he was particularly photogenic.

Anchu went to the boy and his adoptive mother and put my invitation to them. Tadehah said he wanted to come, and the mother sent me a message by Anchu asking me not to take him home to my own mother after the expedition. I promised to bring him back, and on the day we started out, with five Yequana men to help, Tadehah brought his hammock and found himself a seat in one of the canoes.

A disagreement developed about a week later, and the Yequana men suddenly marched out of camp, saying they were going home. They turned at the last moment and said, 'Mahtyeh!' ('Come along!') to Tadehah, whose hammock was still strung in the shelter.

The child only said softly, 'Ahkay' ('No'), and the others went on their way.

There was no attempt to force or even to persuade him to come with them. He belonged, like anyone else, to himself. His decision was an expression of his self-ownership, and its outcome part of his destiny. No one presumed to override his right to decide for himself just because he was small and weak enough to be dominated physically or because his decision-making abilities were less experienced.

Among the Yequana a person's judgement is thought to be adequate to make any decision he feels motivated to make. The impulse to make a decision is evidence of the ability to do it suitably. Small children do *not* make large decisions; they are strongly interested in self-preservation, and in matters beyond their powers of comprehension they look to elders to judge what is best. Leaving the choice to the child from the earliest age keeps his judgement, either to delegate or to make decisions, at peak efficiency. Caution asserts itself in relation to the responsibility involved, and errors are thus kept at an absolute minimum. A decision taken in this way receives no opposition from the child and therefore works with harmony and pleasure for all concerned.

At his age Tadehah was well able to make what seemed to me an enormous commitment for a child. He chose not to go with his tribesmen but to stay with three utterly strange strangers, part-way up a large river with no crew and, because I had not thought of trading for any of our own, no paddles, since the men had left with theirs.

Tadehah knew his own abilities and wanted the adventure. We

all had plenty of that in the months before we came back, but he was always up to it, never anything but helpful and always happy.

The extent of their unwillingness to bring pressure to bear on one another was also impressed upon me on the fourth expedition, when André, a Belgian, and I were detained by Anchu in spite of our wish to leave. It might be as well to explain that this seeming contradiction about the imposition of wills upon other people could be accounted for partly by the fact that the Yequana do not regard us or the Sanema tribes as people, and partly by the fact that the Yequana prevented us from leaving (so that I could continue doctoring them) by the expedient of not accompanying us on the trip out, a trip that two people could not have attempted alone. They fed us and built a hut for us, and our demands that we be taken out were always hedged, never flatly refused. No one, in other words, actually forced us to do anything, except by omitting to aid us.

There were two men, one in the village and one who lived nearby, who were extremely ill. One had appendicitis with complications, and the other had two fistulae in his back. Both were clearly going to die, as weeks and months passed without improvement, despite my managing to keep them alive on antibiotics.

Early in this uphill struggle – the first time, in fact, that I made a 'house call' upriver to see the young man with appendicitis – I told his father that he must be taken to Ciudad Bolivar, to a real doctor, for surgery. I explained that a hole must be cut and the trouble taken out, and I showed him my own appendectomy scar. He agreed but said Masawiu could not go to a Venezuelan town without being able to speak Spanish. He did not directly suggest that I take him, though his only son was very dear to him. He would evidently have let Masawiu die rather than ask me to put myself to any trouble. He had let me know the problem; that was all the persuasion he would use.

I told him I would take his son to be cured but that he must go to Anchu and insist that we be allowed to go immediately. At this the old fellow looked quite blank, though I repeated emphatically that he must speak to Anchu or his son would die. He never did anything like insisting, though he may have mentioned the situation to the chief when he moved his entire family down to the village so that I could treat Masawiu. His relations with Anchu continued to be just as casual as though his son's life were not in the chief's hands.

Four months later, when I was freed at last to make the long, difficult trip out with my patients, the father and all his family came along in a separate canoe to await Masawiu's cure in a nearby river and take him home afterwards. So the old man's refusal to pressure anyone on his behalf was not for lack of caring.

It was the same when I asked Nahakadi, a special friend of mine and a great friend, as well as sister through adoption, of Anchu, to exert pressure upon him to release us in order to take her dying husband to hospital. She saw the chief often and had plenty of opportunity, but always kept her conversations with him light and pleasant, even a few feet from the hammock where her beloved husband lay wasting away and in pain.

She did come to me several times during those months when I was treating him to suggest that I make an incision in his back to drain the fistulae. I declined, for fear of my own ignorance of surgery, and eventually she tried to do the job but could not bring herself to push the fish barb she was using into her husband's back, and she sent their son to call me. When I saw what she was trying to do I promised to do it myself rather than incur the greater risk of her unhygienic method. If she had persuaded me by 'moral blackmail' it worked, but there was no direct bearing of her will on mine.

In the end I got both men to the hospital alive. They survived and were returned to their people.

My own insistence that Anchu let us go fell on deaf ears. He always changed the subject and asked if I did not like the hut they had built for us or the food they gave us. When I told him day after day of the danger of delay to the two men's lives, he answered at last by painting himself, dressing himself in all his beads, and closeting himself with the two men for a week while he chanted to the accompaniment of a rattle in the Yequana shamanic tradition. During his naps others took over the chant. His treatment did not improve the patients, but it kept everyone from thinking that Anchu was careless of the lives of his people. This is not to imply that he was a fake. He was not one of the great Yequana shamans, but he may very well have been doing his best and probably felt it was better in the long run to keep me there to serve all his people as doctor rather than to let me go in an attempt to save two hopeless-looking cases.

The unwillingness of one Yequana ever to cajole another does not seem to be a choice made by the individual. It is apparently a prohibition evolved by the continuum and sustained by their culture. They are very well able to assert force on other species; they train hunting dogs by strict discipline and punishment that includes striking them with fists, sticks and stones and cutting their ears. But they will not impose their wills on their fellow men – not even, as we have seen, on children.

There was an exception that proved the rule, like the playpen incident. I saw a young father lose patience one day with his year-old son. He shouted and made some violent motion as I watched and may even have struck him. The baby screamed with deafening, unmistakable horror. The father stood chastened by the dreadful sound he had caused; it was clear that he had committed an offence against nature. I saw the family often, as I lived next door to them, but I never saw the man lose respect for his son's dignity again.

None the less, the parents' attitude is not a 'permissive' one. While honouring the autonomy of their sons and daughters and assuming that they will behave as social beings, they also set many of the standards to which the children conform.

At mealtimes at the family hearth the appearance, to civilized eyes, is of solemnity, as the mother silently puts the gourds and mats before the father, and the children sit by, eating or handing round food without a word. The mother may say something in her soft little voice; a child will spring to its feet and fetch a gourd for the father or for her. The action is swift, silent and efficient, even when the child is a mere tot. It looked to me like the pared-down action of fear, as though the whole ritual were designed not to antagonize the paterfamilias, who represented a kind of egocentric menace to the others. But it was not so.

On closer observation, all parties were found to be completely relaxed, and the silence harboured no threat, held no charge at all in fact, apart from mutual understanding and trust in the doing of things in the way those things are done. The 'solemnity', when one saw there was no tension in it, was simply peace. The lack of conversation signified the presence of ease among them, not an absence of it. The child or children might have something to say, and would say it without any sign of timidity or shrillness, but usually they did not. It is the Yequana custom to dine with silence 'at the head of the table' for the sake of serenity, and what little anyone says is in keeping with this spirit.

It is the arrival of the father that quietens the woman and children. It is also under the eye of the fathers and men in general that women and children take pride in doing their best, in living up to the men's expectations as well as to one another's. Boys especially like to measure themselves against their fathers, while girls enjoy serving them. It is reward enough for a little girl to be able to bring a fresh piece of cassava to her father and have him take it from her hands. By his behaviour, his own dignity and excellence in what he does, he shows their society's ways to the young. If an infant cries while the men are in a talking session, his mother carries him out of earshot. If he sullies the floor before he is house-trained but old enough to understand, he is told sternly to go outside. He is told not to dirty the floor, but he is not told that he is bad or that he is always doing the wrong thing. He never feels he is bad, only, at most, that he is a loved child doing an undesirable act. The child himself wants to stop doing things distasteful to his people. He is innately social.

If there is any deviation or even an accidental exception to a child's right behaviour, neither the mothers nor the fathers are soft about it. They do not pamper him in the least. Like Anchu during Wididi's crisis, their standards remain steady.

They do not make pitying sounds when a child hurts himself. They wait for him to pick himself up and catch up, if that is all that is needed. In the case of a serious injury or illness they do their best to help towards healing by giving medicaments or by shamanism, sometimes chanting for days and nights on end, addressing themselves to the evil that has entered the body but not expressing sympathy to the patient, who makes peace as best he can with his ailment without disturbing anyone unnecessarily.

When I was there they brought or sent ailing children to me for treatment. On these occasions the very great difference between continuum children and non-continuum children was particularly evident. The Yequana, who had been correctly treated during the in-arms phase, who knew themselves to be lovable, did not seek any extra mothering to offset their pain unless it was excruciating, while our civilized children, each tacitly acknowledged to bear a permanent burden of pain (the longing for more maternal contact than he has had), are given hugs and kisses and fond words for the smallest bumps. Their scraped knees may not be helped, but the total painload is lightened at a moment when it is especially strained.

It may be that expecting sympathy is largely a learned behaviour. I have little doubt that it is, but the self-confidence and trust in others (in this case an outsider) demonstrated by small children who came to me for treatment was indicative of something far more positive than a simple lack of expecting to be pampered.

On an early expedition in Yequana country I was at Wanania, Anchu's village, when a boy of about four came to me. He approached shyly, unsure of his welcome. When our eyes met and a smile had been reassuringly exchanged, he held up his thumb for me to see. He had no self-pity, or bid for pity, on his face, only a brilliant smile. The top of his thumb and part of the nail had been cut through except for a shred of skin that kept it from falling off. Half-dried blood held it together but out of line. As I set about cleaning and realigning it, the pain brought tears to his immense, fawn-like eyes, and sometimes his tiny hand quivered as he held it out to me, but he never pulled back or made more sound than a whimper at especially bad moments; most of the time he was relaxed and his face was in repose. When his thumb was bandaged I pointed to it and said, 'Tuunah, *ah*key!' ('No water!'), and his musical little voice repeated, 'Tuunah *ah*key!' then, 'Hwaynamah ehtah' ('Tomorrow here'), and he went away. All his behaviour contradicted the assumptions I held about how children behave, how they must be handled in emergencies, the importance of reassurance as part of medical treatment and so on. I could hardly believe what I had seen.

On a later trip I was awakened one morning by a *two*-year-old calling in a soft piping tone, 'Si! Si!' It was the best he could do to pronounce 'Shi', my Yequana name. I looked out of my hammock and there was Cananasi, quite alone, with a cut in need of repair. He did not cry at all or require any holding or steadying. He waited until his bandage was in place, listened to my admonition not to put his hand in water and to come back the next day, and ran off to play.

When I caught up with him the following day, his bandage was both wet and dirty. His intellectual comprehension at two was insufficient to effect obedience to an order that had to be remembered all day, but the soundness of his experience of Self and Other during two good years, one of a richly full in-arms phase and one crammed with practice of self-reliance in a challenging world, made him able to come for and accept his treatment without support, sympathy or any but a minimum of notice. I suppose his mother had seen the cut and said only, 'Go to Jean,' and Cananasi had done the rest.

Another incident was full of revelation for me, though it happened after many months of familiarity with the Yequana's casual attitude towards being doctored. Awadahu, Anchu's second son, who was about nine, arrived alone at my hut with a wound in his abdomen. It turned out not to be dangerously deep, but at first glance I was afraid of the harm it might do in so vulnerable a spot. 'Nehkuhmuhduh?' ('What was it?') I asked.

'Shimada,' ('An arrow') he said politely.

'Amahday?' ('Yours?') I pursued.

'Katawehu,' he said, naming his ten-year-old brother with as much emotion as if I had asked him the name of a flower.

As I worked on the frightening-looking wound, Katawehu and some other boys stopped in to see what I was doing. There was no evidence of guilt in Katawehu or any of anger in Awadahu. It was simply an accident. Their mother came up, asked what had happened and was told in brief terms that her eldest son had shot an arrow into her second son at the riverbank.

'Yeheduhmuh?' ('Really?') she said softly.

Before I finished she had left the group of onlookers to continue about her chores. Her son was being looked after without having called upon her; there was no need for her to stay. The only person who was at all worried was I. What had been done had been done; the best care available was being given, and there was no need even for the other boys to wait until I had finished before running off again to play. Awadahu needed no moral support, and when I had put the last plaster on he went back to the river to join them.

His mother assumed that if he needed her, he would come to her, and she was available for any such eventuality.

My mentioning these incidents might give the false impression that the Yequana have many accidents. By comparison with their

Western civilized, middle-class contemporaries they have remark-ably few. It is no coincidence that those Westerners are perhaps the most carefully protected children in history as regards external safeguards and are therefore the least *expected* to know how to look after themselves.

A case in point is one American family I heard of who were nervous of the danger their swimming pool presented to their small child. The idea was not that the pool would rise up and swallow the child but that the child might fall or throw himself into the pool. They had a fence built around the pool and kept its gate locked.

Very possibly the logical mind of the child (not the part that reasons), assisted by explanations from his parents, grasped the suggestion of the fence and the locked gate. He comprehended so well what was expected of him that, finding the gate open one day, he entered, fell into the pool and drowned.

When I heard this story, which was told me to show that children need constant guarding from their own ability to harm themselves, I could not help thinking of that pit in the compound at Wanania where the children played unsupervised all day without incident. These two isolated cases do not mean much, of course, but they do represent quite accurately a difference in the two cultures. There are many more potentially dangerous situations among the Yequana. One of the most striking is the omnipresence of machetes and knives, all razor-sharp and all available to step on, fall against or play with. Babies, too young to have learned about handles, picked them up by the blades and, as I watched, waved them about in their dimpled fists. They not only did not sever their own fingers or injure themselves at all, but if they were in their mothers' arms, they managed to miss hurting them either.

Similarly, a baby playing with a firebrand, stumbling and falling with it, and climbing in and out of his house with it over a foot-high doorsill, never actually touched the wood, or the overhanging palm thatch, or his own hair or anyone else's. Babies, like puppies, played about beside the family fire without interference from their respective elders.

The boys, from the age of about eighteen months, practised archery with sharp arrows, some enthusiasts carrying their bows and arrows about most of their waking hours. Shooting was not confined to designated places, nor were any 'safety rules' in effect. In my two and a half years there I saw only the one arrow wound I have mentioned.

There are the hazards of the jungle, including the great ease with which one can lose oneself in its trackless vastness and the chances of injuring one's bare feet and naked body while walking, besides more noted dangers like snakes, scorpions or jaguars.

And there are the rivers, in which rapids are even more frequent and perilous than anacondas or crocodiles, and a child swimming farther out in the current than his strength and ability allow has a good chance of being smashed on the rocks or against one of many submerged branches. The depth and swiftness of a familiar part of the river vary enormously from day to day according to the amount of rainfall upstream, so knowing the dangers one day may not be useful the next. The children who bathe and play in the river every day must gauge their ability accurately under all conditions.

The operative factor seems to be placement of responsibility. In most Western children the machinery for looking after themselves is in only partial use, a great deal of the burden having been assumed by adult caretakers. With its characteristic abhorrence of redundancy, the continuum withdraws as much self-guardianship as is being taken over by others. The result is diminished efficiency because no one can be as constantly or as thoroughly alert to anyone else's circumstances as one is oneself. It is another instance of trying to better nature, another example of mistrust of faculties not intellectually controlled and usurpation of their functions by the intellect, which does not have the capacity to take all relevant information into consideration.

Besides causing civilized children to have more accidents, this propensity of ours to interfere with nature's placement of responsibility where it works best also gives rise to innumerable other hazards. A notable example is the accidental setting of fires.

In a Midwestern American city one winter not long ago there was a blizzard that completely stopped traffic, and therefore the movement of fire engines, for several days. Accustomed to dealing with an average of forty-odd fires a day, the fire chief appeared on television to beg people to take extra care not to start fires during the emergency. He advised them that they would have to cope with any fires themselves. As a consequence the daily average dropped to four fires until the streets were cleared, at which time the number increased to normal.

It cannot be imagined that many of the forty normal daily fires were set on purpose, but those who accidentally brought them about were evidently aware that great care was not really necessary when the fire brigade was quick and efficient. Apprised of the change in placement of responsibility, they unconsciously cut the figure by 90 per cent.

Similarly, Tokyo has a permanently smaller incidence of fires than most large cities, apparently because many of the houses are built of wood and paper and fire would spread with disastrous speed, while the fire-fighting equipment would have exceptional difficulty in moving through the very crowded streets. The citizens are familiar with the conditions and behave accordingly.

This placement of responsibility is an aspect of expectation, the force that can be seen to assert its power in so much of child and adult behaviour. How could we be described as social creatures if we did not have a strong proclivity for behaving as we feel we are expected to?

For anyone wishing to apply continuum principles in civilized life, this change-over to trust in children's self-protective ability is one of the most difficult problems. We are so unaccustomed to it that leaving our children to their own devices, on the theory that they will be better off without our vigilance, is more than many people could do. Most of us would at least steal apprehensive glances at them, risking being caught at it and having the look taken for an expectation of inefficiency. And what would give us the faith necessary to let a baby play with a really sharp knife, the faith the Yequana have come by through long experience? It is not their experience of babies with knives, for the introduction of metal has been very recent, but familiarity with the ability of babies to sense the subtlest factors in their surroundings and conduct themselves safely among them.

We have no choice but to find our way back to that knowledge common to the Yequana and our own ancestors *through* the use of the intellect. It is not very different from asking oneself to go to church and pray for belief in God; one would have to do one's best to act as though one believed first. Some will be better actors and actresses than others; but if each anxious parent allows a little more trust in the baby's instinct for self-preservation than he or she would have had before, consequent experience of the baby's ability will permit ever more trust.

Language is the newest of the major developments in the amazing catalogue of animal capabilities. The ability to form a succession of concepts of increasing complexity is reflected in the verbal abilities of a developing child. His view of the universe, and the relationship of Self to Other, necessarily changes with that development and his time-conditioned concept of time.

As a consequence, there is a conceptual gap between age groups. Notwithstanding the recent fashion for talking things over and 'reasoning' with children, there remains a quite unbridgeable gulf between what is meant or understood by the six-year-old in his universe and what is meant or understood by a thirty-year-old in his. Language is of limited value in their association.

Among the Yequana it is interesting to note that there is only a very basic 'Wait here' or 'Hand me that' sort of verbal communication between adults and children. There is a stratified system of conversation that consists of total verbal exchanges by children of approximately the same age with diminishing communication as age differs. There is minimal chat between the boys and the girls whose lives and interests are so very different from one another's, and seldom, even as adults, do they seem to have occasion for long talks between the sexes.

When adults converse, children generally listen. They do not talk among themselves. At no time is a person of any age called upon to use a false point of view, as we and our children do when speaking with one another. Yequana adults say anything they have to say in front of the children, and the children listen, comprehending the proceedings according to their abilities. When the time comes for a child to join the adults he has grown to understand their speech and patterns and point of view at his own pace, without the necessity of having to discredit a series of patterns and points of view confected by them for children.

Each age group grasps the conceptual structures appropriate to its development, following in the footsteps of the children a little older than themselves until they have a full complement of verbal (and cultural) thought forms able to take in adult views and the whole content that has been available to them since their infancy.

Our own system of trying to guess what or how much a child's mind can assimilate results in cross purposes, misunderstanding, disappointments, anger and a general loss of harmony. The disastrous custom of teaching children that 'good' will always be rewarded and 'evil' always punished, that promises are always kept, that grown-ups never tell lies and so on not only necessitates slapping them down later for being 'unrealistic' and 'immature' if they have by chance gone on believing the nursery fictions, but also creates a sense of disillusionment that usually applies itself to their upbringing in general and what they *believed* to be the culture they were expected to follow. The results are confusion about how to behave, as the basis for action is snatched away, and suspicion of anything else their culture tells them.

Again it is the intellect trying to 'decide' what a child can understand, when the continuum way simply permits the child to absorb what he can from the total verbal environment, which is undistorted and unedited. It is impossible to hurt the mind of a child with concepts it cannot understand as long as that mind is allowed to leave what it cannot digest. But taking a child by the shoulders and trying to force him to understand can create a sad conflict between what he can comprehend and what he feels is expected of him. Allowing children to listen freely and understand what they can eliminates any suggestion about how much is expected and obviates that ruinous conflict.

While Yequana girls spend much of their childhood with the women, participating from the first in their work at home or in the gardens, boys run about together most of the time; their fathers can allow them to come along only when speed and endurance are not essential. In the meantime the little boys are shooting a thousand shots at grasshoppers or, later, at little birds, while a man out hunting may shoot only once or twice all day, giving little chance for a boy to develop his skill, except at finding and retrieving game.

Both boys and girls go swimming almost every day. In canoeing too they are expert incredibly early, guiding heavy dugouts through tricky currents and rapids, sometimes with no one in the crew over six or seven years old. Boys and girls often paddle canoes together. There is no sort of taboo on their association, only a usual lack of coincidence of activities.

At the same time each Yequana child, free of the need for reassurance, is well able to do things on his or her own. Fishing is often done alone by a member of either sex, child or adult. Basketry and weapon making and repairing are done by boys and men, working alone. Hammering the teeth into cassava graters, weaving armbands or hammocks and cooking are done by women and girls, very often in solitude or with only an infant as companion.

But the Yequana never permit themselves to suffer boredom or loneliness. The great majority of their time is spent in the company of their peers. Men often hunt and do certain kinds of fishing, some stages of canoe making and house building together. They go on trading trips in groups, and several at a time slash and burn the areas where they plant their gardens. Women and girls walk to the gardens and go through the processes of making cassava, fetching water and firewood and so on in groups. Boys practise shooting arrows and blowing darts, play games, swim, explore or gather food, usually in groups. Men, women, girls, boys or families, when doing things together, all talk a great deal with high spirits and good humour. Laughter is impressively frequent, and the young men often whoop joyously in chorus at the end of a good story, piece of news or joke. This party atmosphere is the everyday norm. Their parties, in fact, do not do much to improve on the customary high level of fun.

One of the most striking differences between the Yequana and any other children I have seen is that the former neither fight nor argue among themselves. There is no competitiveness, and leadership is established on the initiative of the followers. In the years I spent with them I never saw a child argue with another, much less fight. The only angry words I did hear were two or three bursts of impatience from an adult with an undesirable act done by a child. Then a little tirade of complaint was hurled at him as he stood looking concerned or hurried to mend the error, and when the matter was put right no grudge was borne by the child or by the adult.

Although I have seen many a party at which every Yequana,

man, woman and child was drunk, I have never seen even the beginnings of an altercation, which makes one think that they really are as they look – in harmony with one another and happily at home in their own skins.

5 : Deprivation of Essential Experiences

Civilized life cannot be viewed usefully without taking into constant consideration the fact that we have been deprived of almost all the in-arms experience and much of the later experience we expected, and that we go on, in an orderly but unconscious way, seeking the fulfilment of those expectations in their unalterable sequence.

We are disengaged from our human continuum at birth, left starving for experience in cots and prams, away from the stream of life. Parts of us remain infantile and cannot contribute positively to our lives as older children and adults. But we do not, we cannot, leave them behind. The want of in-arms experience remains alongside the development of mind and body, waiting to be fulfilled.

We in civilization share certain ailments of the continuum. Self-hate and self-doubt are quite general among us, in varying degrees, depending upon how and when the complex of deprivations affected our inherited qualities. The quest for in-arms experience, as the years pass and we grow up, takes on a great many forms. Loss of the essential condition of well-being that should have grown out of one's time in arms leads to searches and substitutions for it. *Happiness ceases to be a normal condition of being alive, and becomes a goal*. The goal is pursued in short- and long-term ways.

Bearing in mind the lives of the Yequana, it becomes increasingly clear why we do many of the seemingly pointless things we do.

In-arms deprivation expresses itself perhaps most commonly as an underlying feeling of unease in the here and now. One feels off-centre, as though something were missing; there is a vague sense of loss, of wanting something one cannot define. The wanting often attaches itself to an object or event in the middle distance; put into words, it would be 'I'd be all right if only ...', followed by some proposed change, like having a new suit, a new car, a promotion or rise in salary, a different job, a chance to go away either for a holiday or permanently, or a man or woman or child to love if one does not already have one.

When the object is attained, the middle distance, where mother once was, is soon occupied by a new 'if only', and the distance between it and oneself becomes the new measure of the space between oneself and the missing rightness – rightness in the here and now.

One is sustained by the hopes raised by the succession of objects as they arise at the distance dictated by the degree of unattainableness one needs in order to feel 'at home', that is, in the same relationship as one was in to one's mother when in-arms experience was denied.

Difficulty in keeping objects at the necessary distance can lead to disaster. It does not happen often, as most people can easily imagine a constant parade of things they cannot have, no matter what they do have. But occasionally the imagination is outstripped by too rapid or complete an attainment of the goals it is able to set.

Not many years ago a famous blonde film star became the victim of what was apparently an unbearable imbalance between her need to hope and things left to hope for. She was the world's most successful actress, the world's most desired woman. She had reached for, married and divorced men of notable physical and intellectual achievement. By the standards of her imagination she had all she wanted. Bewildered at not having achieved the missing feeling of rightness, she searched the horizon for something desirable that she could not immediately have and, failing, could no longer sustain hope of relief and committed suicide.

Many another girl and woman, whose goals had been similar to hers, asked how-could-she-who-had-everything? But damage to that quarter of the American Dream was not serious, for in her heart each wondering woman was certain that if only ... if only *she* had so many desirable things of life, she who felt happiness already not very far out of her reach, she would not fail to be happy.

There is no shortage of examples of similarly inspired suicides, but far more common is the desperate behaviour of the successful, whose instinct for self-preservation prevents the ultimate step into oblivion, but whose lives are full of heavy drinking, drug taking, divorce and melancholy. Most rich people can and do long to be richer; those with power want more power and their longing is thereby given form. It is the few who have come to the end, or within sight, of all they had it in them to want who have to face the unsatisfiable quality of their longing. They cannot remember its original form: their craving as infants for their place in their mothers' arms. To all intents and purposes they are staring into a bottomless abyss, asking and receiving no answer about the point of it all, when once they may have been quite sure it was money, fame, or achievement.

Marriage in civilized life has become a double contract in many cases; one clause might read: '... and I'll be your mother if you'll be my mother'. The ever-present infantile needs of each partner are expressed when the implicit (often explicit) declaration is, 'I love you, I want you, and I need you.' The first two-thirds of this speech are appropriate to mature men and women, but customarily the notion of needing, though it is romantically acceptable in our culture, implies a requirement for a certain amount of babying. It can range from baby talk ('Does ums love little me?') to a tacit agreement not to pay more than superficial attention to other persons. Often the dominant need is to be the object of attention (continuation of the cries for attention that were to effect one's transferral into the centre of life but, unheeded, eventually came to be only an endless craving for attention itself) and the partners may come to a fairly amicable division of stage-centre.

Courtship is often a testing ground to determine how far each partner's infantile needs will be met. For people with extensive requirements – people whose early lives have left them without enough fulfilment even to compromise satisfactorily with another person and his needs – the search for a mate is often a sad and endless one. Betrayed in infancy, their longings are wide and deep. The fear of being betrayed again can be so strong that the moment there is danger of finding a companion, they flee in terror to avoid putting the candidate to the test and being reminded, unbearably, that they are not lovable in the unconditional way they require.

Innumerable men and women have found themselves victims of a 'pattern' of behaviour in courtship that demonstrates a dread of happiness with no apparent explanation. Even when it is fairly easy to overcome the fear of finding a mate, bridegrooms balk at the altar and brides still weep with anxiety when the time comes to step forward and claim their happiness. But many go on for years, changing partners, looking for a relationship they cannot name, unable to commit themselves to anyone so paltry as a man or woman no bigger or more important than themselves.

The difficulty in finding an acceptable mate has been complicated further by cultural images such as the love objects produced by films, television, novels, magazines and advertisements. The cinematic spectator-dwarfing images create an illusion of being the long-lost 'right' or mother-sized people. We have an unreasoning trust of these huge creatures, and we endow the actors themselves with the aura of perfection that clings to them in our minds. They can do no wrong, they are above judgements of the sort we make upon one another. And to make matters more confusing, the characters they represent, however unrealistic, set standards for our desires that make real people seem more inadequate than ever.

Advertising has learned to capitalize on the longings of the in-arms-deprived public by holding out promises that seem to say, 'If you had this you would feel right again.' A soft drink is sloganed 'It's the real thing'. Its main rival appeals to the missing sense of belonging with 'You're in the Pepsi generation' or with pictures of 'right'-looking 'Pepsi people'. One company suggests an end to longing with 'A diamond is for ever'. The implication is that ownership of a thing of guaranteed value will give oneself a value of the same permanence, unassailability, and absoluteness. It is as though one did not have to be lovable to be loved if one is wearing a diamond, a magic ring that attracts all persons at all times. Status furs and cars, a good address and so on also seem to attract the acceptance one longs for. At the same time, they surround one with security amid uncertainty, not unlike the encircling arms one has always missed. Whatever our culture holds out as the right thing to have, to be 'inside' is what we want, for we feel chronically outside, though we try for ever to tell ourselves that we are 'in', even while making new efforts to make ourselves believe it.

Although most of us cannot remember ever feeling thoroughly right, truly inside the moment as it is lived, we do often transfer the illusion of it to the past as well as to the future. We speak of the golden days of childhood, or the good old days, to sustain the illusion that rightness is not really far away. The innocence of childhood, which we think protected us from the cruel realities, was accompanied by bewilderment and confusion at the contradictions between what we were told and what we saw happening, and the sense of something missing was always there, then as now, but the illusion then was that we would be let in on rightness when we grew up and joined the people of the 'right' age.

Little did we suspect that the people of the right age would always remain one jump ahead of us until time permitted us to believe that they were now one jump, or more, behind us.

The notion that fulfilment, the feeling of rightness, comes through competing and winning is an extension of what Freud called 'sibling rivalry'. It seemed to him that all of us had to cope with jealousy and hatred of our brothers and sisters, who threatened our access to our mothers. But Freud had no undeprived people in his acquaintance. If he had had the opportunity to know the Yequana, he would have found that the idea of competing and winning, as an end in itself, is quite unknown to them. It cannot therefore be considered an intrinsic part of the human personality. When a baby has had all he needs of experience in his mother's arms and parts with her of his own free will, it makes him able to welcome with no difficulty the advent of a new baby in the place he has voluntarily left. There is no ground for rivalry when nothing he requires is being usurped.

Among the Yequana, there is a variety of motives for wanting things and people, but simply winning out over others is not one of them. They have no competitive games, though there are games. There is wrestling, but there is no championship, only a series of matches between pairs of men. The constant practice of archery is always aimed at achieving excellence but never in competition with other boys, nor is hunting a competitive matter among men. Their emotional life does not require it, so their culture does not provide it. It is difficult for us to imagine life without competition – as difficult as it is to imagine feeling right just as we are.

The same could be said of the pursuit of novelty. It is so much a part of the present phase in our culture that our natural resistance to change has been distorted. It almost appears that it has been turned into a compulsion to change with a frequency so regular as to approach monotony or changelessness.

The idea has sprung up very recently that the newest way must be the best. Advertising has taken charge of fostering the novelty race. There is no rest, no respite. Nothing is ever allowed to be good enough, nothing ever satisfactory. Our underlying discontent is channelled into desire for the latest things.

Among the things high on the list are those that save labour. In the labour-saving device the attraction is doubled, fed by two aspects of in-arms deprivation. The first, to acquire something 'right', is reinforced by the second, to obtain the greatest amount of well-being with the least effort. In a continuum-complete person, the infant's ability to get what he wants without doing anything gives way to a growing desire to exercise his capacity for work. When success as a passive baby has not been experienced, there is a penchant for button-pushing, for labour-saving, as an assurance that everything is being done for, and nothing expected of, the subject. The act of pushing the button is akin to giving a signal to one's caretaker but this time can be done with confidence that one's wish will be granted. The impulse to work, necessarily a strong one in a healthy continuum, is stunted; it cannot develop properly in the barren soil of unreadiness to take care of oneself. Work becomes what it is to most of us: a resented necessity. And the labour-saving gadget gleams with a promise of lost comfort. In the meantime, a solution to the discrepancy between the adult desire to utilize one's abilities and the infantile desire to be useless is often found in something aptly called recreation.

A man who spends his necessary, unenjoyed working life among papers and ideas will re-create his innate expectation of physical work through something like golf. Unmindful that its main virtue is uselessness, the golfer trudges about in the sun carrying a heavy load of clubs and every so often brings his attention to a sharp focus on the problem of persuading a ball to fall into a hole in the ground; this is done, very inefficiently, with the end of one of the clubs, not by carrying the ball and dropping it in. If he were made to do all this by force, he would feel sorely put upon, but as it is called recreation and is guaranteed to serve no purpose beyond exercising him, he is free to enjoy it as the Yequana enjoy useful work.

But there are now many golfers who have allowed the labour-saving impulse to spoil some of this pleasure as well, since it has been suggested by the relevant sector of the culture that carrying the clubs is not pleasant and, more recently, that the trudging between strokes ought also to be moved into the work category and little automotive carts used instead. To re-create themselves after playing golf, they may soon have to resort to tennis.

The continuing need for the missed experiences of the in-arms phase leads us to some very bizarre behaviour. It would not be easy to account for our taste for roller coasters, loop-the-loops and Ferris wheels, were it not for the fact that we have an unfilled quota of time in a situation of reliable safety with sudden changes of position surrounded by looming dangers. The attraction of any animal to being buffeted about and frightened can be explained only by discovering what need it could fill. The millions of years of cosy thrills experienced by infants in arms as their mothers leaped about in trees, on savannas, in water or wherever must be missed by the late unfortunates who have only the silence and immobility of a cot or the well-sprung and padded motion of a pram plus a little knee-bouncing and if they are lucky, some tossing into the air by fathers still able to hear the voice of their own continua.

The secret of the attraction is in the safety zone, the strapped-in seat in the little car as it races and plunges along the track or high in the air. It is the pleasure of being safe amid what would *otherwise* be frightening circumstances. The 'tunnel of love' has ghosts and skeletons popping out and giving us frights that we can enjoy while we know we are safe; it is the understanding under which we buy our tickets.

The same is true of the enormously popular monster thriller film that we watch from a seat from which we are sure to emerge unscathed. If the theatre were actually subject to a visit by a loose gorilla, dinosaur, or vampire, there would be little demand for tickets.

The infant's business in arms is to have experiences that will ready him for further development towards self-reliance. The witnessing of, and passive participation in, those startling, violent and menacing events that are the daily lot of a babe in the arms of a busy mother are essential building blocks for confidence in himself. It is an important part of the stuff of which the sense of self is made.

In a milder way, riding on horses, rocking or real, in cars, toy or real, and in or on anything else that carries us, adds to our missed quota of *that* aspect of in-arms experience and lessens our measure of need for it. Riding is often addictive, for as soon as many of us discover the pleasure of being carried by a horse or motorcar, we have a feeling of let-down when left again to our own feet; but let us consider the role of addiction later.

Expressions of in-arms deprivation chequer our lives and colour the personalities around us so frequently that we tend to view them as part of human nature. An example is the 'Casanova syndrome', which compels a man to try to show himself that he is lovable by making up in numbers of conquests what is missing in the special quality of love that should have been found in his mother, the kind that assures one of one's existence and one's worth. The collecting of testimonies to his lovableness does go some way towards replacing the missing conviction. In each moment in the arms of each lady a little is made up, and eventually the unsatisfiable Casanova 'tires' of that brand of search for the feeling of rightness and is able to contemplate a more advanced, more mature position towards women. In most Casanovas this occurs reasonably early in life, but some cases can never free themselves of the illusion that sexual conquest is a point on the right scoreboard and that perfecting the conquering technique is the road to restoring what is mysteriously lacking in life.

Gigolos and gold-diggers believe that the money value associated with the women or men they win is the true measure of their own value and usually feel that marriage to a rich person will make them rich and therefore incontestably acceptable as well. Somehow they have been given the impression that money equals love in this way in addition to the more commonly held illusion that money equals happiness. The cultural influences that perpetuate these fallacies are not difficult to discover. But removal of the fallacious suggestion as to the whereabouts of lovableness or happiness would not solve the difficulty. The sense of lack of rightness would only find some other hope upon which to pin itself and the chances are strong that it would be an equally illusory one.

'Slob syndrome' is another common manifestation of deprivation in infancy. The slob, like the drooling, tousled baby, wants to be loved simply because he exists and precludes his having done anything to qualify the feelings towards him by pleasing behaviour.

He smacks his lips to make himself feel that anyone who is near him is glad to know he is enjoying his food; he imposes his physical presence wherever he can, leaving ash or stains or litter to bear witness to his existence, challenging all present to reject him and his right to be loved. As he finds he is rejected, he then reinforces his sad statement to the mother cosmos: 'You see? No one loves me because you don't bother to wipe my chin!' And he barges on his way, unwashed, unkempt and accidentally stepping on everyone's toes. His hope is that the mother cosmos will, as a mother absolutely must (his continuum says so), take pity on him for all he has suffered and welcome him at last to her unconditional love. He will never close the door on her return by doing his grooming himself; it would constitute an admission of hopelessness.

Not unlike the slob is the martyr, who suffers accusingly too, but with a great emphasis on the amount of suffering that *must* eventually be recompensed. Bright-eyed figures have marched staunchly to trenches, pyres, gallows and lions' jaws for any number of causes. Giving their all, they feel, must surely earn them their rightful place at last. The advantage is that ultimate sacrificers do not return to complain that they have been cheated, so the illusion remains safe for those who are so inclined, perhaps by an early history with a mother who was given to extravagant signs of remorse when baby hurt himself.

The actor personality very often feels the need to be on stage or attended by large numbers of people to prove that he *is* rightly the centre of attention, in spite of his nagging feeling to the contrary; hence, his unremitting need to occupy that position. Pathological exhibitionism and narcissism can be even more desperate bids for this essential attention, when it has consistently been signalled for in vain at the beginning of life. Often it can be seen that a 'close' relationship between the mother and the future 'show-off' actually consisted in the mother trying to win the centre of attention from the baby as a result of her own urgent leftover need.

The compulsive academic, the endless taker of degrees and lifelong inhabitant of colleges in one capacity or another, has made of the alma mater a fairly adaptable mother surrogate. The institution is bigger and more stable than he. It rewards good and bad behaviour quite predictably. It protects from the cold, hard world outside, which is too risky for the inadequate emotional equipment of a deprived infant grown up. The adult desire to test oneself against the world's challenges, and thus to further one's development, cannot come into being in the unassured personality, no matter what its age.

Apparently opposite to the academic who clings to his infant position *vis-à-vis* the school (and the businessman who clings for decades to the petticoats of a corporation) is the adventurer-*conquistador* who has been given the impression, perhaps by a parent, that the way to acceptance is through climbing the highest mountain or sailing the ocean single-handed in a peanut-shell: the unique accomplishment, promising the defeat of all rivals for attention. The acclaim always available to anyone who will stay longer than anyone else on a flagpole, or be the first white man to go somewhere, or cross a waterfall on a tightrope, looks very like what one wants – until, of course, it is attained and found inadequate and a new project is proposed that looks like the real thing, the answer, the passport into rightness.

The compulsive traveller has very much the same sort of sustaining illusion. New places hold the promise of being the right place, for the illusion of the magic return to arms is untenable in any clearly perceived reality. Thus the comparative greenness of far fields gleams alluringly to the if-onlyist, who believes, for reasons not recalled even by himself, that fulfilment lies in the change to a certain other place.

Consistent with the nature of the human continuum and its aeons of experience, the desire to be right on centre in life seems to be a proof that that centre is available. It is part of the design that the missed fulfilment retain its place in the future; in this way only can it serve as motivation towards completion of development. This belief, unimpeded by reason or lessons learned from personal experience, lures us ahead as it is meant to do, no matter how out of context, no matter how behind schedule. If-onlyism of one kind or another accounts for an enormous quantum of the motive power operative among civilized people.

Sadder perhaps to contemplate are those with expressions of deprivation that perpetuate their pain in others. Battered children are among the more obvious of a multitude of sufferers at the hands of deprived and suffering parents.

Professor C. Henry Kempe, chairman of the Department of Pediatrics at Colorado Medical Center, found from his research among 1,000 families that 20 per cent of women have difficulty in 'turning on mothering'. 'A lot of mothers don't love their babies very much,' he said.* His unfortunate interpretation of the figures was that, since so many mothers were unable to love their children, mother love as a natural instinct must be 'a myth' (see page 70). His message was that it is a mistake to expect every mother to be a madonna, all-giving and protecting towards her child, and he blamed the Old Masters for brainwashing people into believing she ought to be. His findings, nevertheless, speak for themselves about baby battering. 'All research points to one irrefutable fact: battered children become battering parents.' And among the circumstances found to produce this form of brutality in parents was that somehow, since they were children themselves, they had 'missed out on mothering' all along the line, by the right teacher, friends, lovers, husband or wife.

'The parent,' says Kempe, 'who lacks mothering herself is incapable of mothering her child but expects the child to be capable of loving her; she expects far more than a baby is capable of and she sees its crying as rejection.' He quoted an intelligent, educated mother saying, 'When he cried, it meant he didn't love me, so I hit him.'

The expectation that her search for love will be rewarded at last by her own love-needy infant is the tragedy of many a woman. And of course it is a looming factor in the quality of deprivation suffered by the child. Not only is a great deal of the necessary loving and attention denied, but the child is competing for it against a bigger, stronger person. What could be more pathetic than a child crying for want of mothering and the mother striking out at it because it is not mothering her in answer to *her* longing?

No one wins in such a game; no one is the villain. All one can discover from horizon to horizon are victims of victims.

Burned children are a more indirect expression of the deprivation in parents. The cases are usually labelled accidental, but Helen L. Martin, a researcher at the Burns Unit of London's Hospital for Sick

* C. H. Kempe and R. Helfer (eds.), *Helping the Battered Child and His Family*, Oxford and New York, 1972.

Children, finds that they are not. She studied fifty cases over seven months and concluded that most burns are actually the result of 'emotional problems'. Except in five instances, she found that the burns had occurred during conflict situations: either tension in the mother, between the child and some other member of the family, or between hostile adults. Tellingly, only two of the burnings took place when the child was alone.

In contrast to batterers, parents who cause their children to be burned are not overtly giving in to their wish to hurt them. They are at cross purposes between their infantile anger and frustration and their parental feelings of protectiveness. Unconsciously using the weapon of expectation to suggest to the child that he burn himself, and perhaps helping by leaving the boiling soup in an unusually reachable position as a further suggestion, the unhappy mother can preserve the necessary virtuous front and at the same time punish herself with guilt in an effort to make it possible for the outraged parent to live in the same skin with the hate-ridden, destructive child she also is.

Lack of 'mothering' from their husbands at the time of their children's accidents was apparent in nearly half the mothers who characterized their attitudes towards their men as 'distant, indifferent, or hostile'. In a control group of families of the same age and background, Helen Martin found only three in the fifty who felt that way.

There is evidence that the strong current of demand for love and attention coming from mother to son can, in its overpowering of the baby's demand, be the cause of homosexuality in his later life. The mother, regarded as possessive or over-attentive, is in fact not *giving* love in her concentrated efforts to win her child's undivided interest; she is demanding it. She often plays the role of 'little girl', and tries to beguile her child with infantile cues into paying attention to her or feeling sorry for her. Unable to prevail against her pull on him, the child's pull upon *her* goes unnoticed, unanswered, and he cannot free himself of his need to get her attention directed at his own lovableness. He grows up feeling that playing the pouting, flouncy little girl's role is the way to win. He plays it against his mother's similar effort and, even as an adult, finds himself magnetized by his seemingly available mother, who protests her love and selfless adoration for him while actually draining him of every bit of attention *he* can give as a growing child and adult.

Having learned in this way that there is no love to be got from the female of the species, but instead that males are the ones who give mothering, they turn for love to males, and often find themselves attracted to very young ones, like the boys they themselves were when their mothers demanded, and got, most intensive mothering from them.

The relationship is then often one of competing for mothering. The homosexual male does not imitate the female adult when he 'camps', but *the female child his mother played to him*. Maturer aspects of adult love are often missing, and the homosexual couple finds difficulty in making an alliance of the sort that deepens with time.

Exceptions are often men who have been blocked away from women for other reasons, such as continuing horror stories about the evils of women told them from an early age. These can come from mothers who are otherwise fairly motherly in their attentions to their sons.

Female homosexuals often feel blocked against the possibility of receiving love from males by cruel or unloving fathers. If they grew up in the presence of a mother whose longing for male attention was a strong factor in her inattention to them, they may behave in a masculine manner because it seems to them the winner's role.

Research into these possibilities might be of substantial value in understanding and treating the unhappiness involved.

Criminality, when it is a pathological personality trait, may also be traced to an unwillingness to play by adult rules, to earn one's share as an equal among adults. The thief may be unable to bear working for the things he needs and wants, feeling that he must somehow obtain them as from a mother, unpaid for. The fact that he often goes to great trouble to get very little 'free' is of no account; the important thing is that in the end he feels he has got 'something for nothing' from the cosmic mother.

The need for punishment, or personal attention, as it may appear to the criminal, is often a part of his infantile relationship to society, from which he steals things of value, signs of love it is unwilling to give him.

These phenomena are not unfamiliar to students of civilized

behaviour but, seen as manifestations of the interrupted continuum, they may take on clearer meaning.

Physical illness, which can be understood as an organism's attempt to restabilize after or during an attack upon it, can accordingly have a variety of roles to play. As we have seen earlier, one of these is the 'righting' effect that punishment has upon the unbearable pain of guilt.

In times of particular emotional need, the continuum can arrange for us to be ill and dependent upon care from others – the kind of care we find it difficult to get as adults in good health. The need for attention can be attached to a special person or to a circle of family and friends or to the hospital system. A hospital, though it may seem impersonal, does put the patient in an infant role, and even if understaffed and inadequate, takes the responsibility for feeding and making decisions for him, a situation not unlike the treatment he might have had in infancy at the hands of a negligent mother. Though not necessarily all he needs, it may be the closest thing available.

At Montefiore Hospital's Loeb Center for Nursing and Rehabilitation in New York, there have been some discoveries that make a great deal of sense from the continuum viewpoint. The Center claimed in 1966 to have cut down the rate of readmission by 80 per cent by an approach of 'acceptance' and encouraging the patients to talk about their problems. Lydia Hall, the registered nurse who was the Center's director and founder, said that the nursing care was equivalent to the care a mother gives a newborn child. 'We answer the patient's demands at once,' she said, 'no matter how trivial they may seem.'

With apparent insight into the tendency to revert, or regress, to an infantile emotional position under stress, Genrose Alfano, the Center's assistant director, said, 'Many people get sick because of their inability to cope with their lives. When they learn how to problem-solve on their own, they don't have to get sick.'

Before becoming ill, of course, most of the patients were coping with their own problems one way or another, but when things became too much for them, like Awadahu holding on to his mother when he came to me with his toothache or the gangrene victim recruiting his wife to see him through his ordeal, they had to have support. Using this motherly technique, the Center has found that recovery is faster too. Miss Hall said fractured hips, a common ailment, heal in half the normal time for a person's age and overall condition. Most patients stay in bed for three weeks after a heart attack, but according to Dr Ira Rubin, a cardiologist, those at the Loeb Center were sufficiently recovered to be on their feet after the second week.

'You take an older person who is out of contact, put him in a social environment where people are interested, where he can talk about his family problems, he gets his muscle tone back faster,' Dr Rubin said.

In a study of 250 patients selected at random, it was shown that only 3.6 per cent of the Center's patients had to be readmitted within a twelve-month period, compared with 18 per cent of those who received home care. It is not difficult to interpret these figures as evidence that care that is more deliberately motherlike fulfils more efficiently the emotional need that brought the patient to illness and hospitalization. Supplying the experiential deficiency shortens the need to be dependent and gives the strength required to return to whatever rate of forward motion one can normally maintain as an adult, or as a child.

Of all the expressions of in-arms deprivation, perhaps research will confirm that one of the most direct is addiction to narcotics like heroin. Only research will be able to ascertain the precise relationship between deprivation and addiction, and when it does, the many forms of addiction – to alcohol, tobacco, gambling, barbiturates or nail biting – may begin to make sense in the light of the continuum concept of human requirements.

But, for the sake of simplicity, let us here consider only the heroin addict. Heroin is chemically addictive in that it creates in the body of the user a demand for more, and that effect diminishes with use, so that more and more of the drug produces less and less the effect desired. Eventually, the addict seeks the drug less to experience the 'high' than to ward off the symptoms of withdrawal. Trying to keep ahead of the tightening circle of demand and use, addicts are sometimes driven to the fatal overdose.

More often, they deliberately confront the agonies of withdrawal in order to 'get clean', free of the increasing chemical imbalance caused by use. They free themselves of the physical dependence over and over again so as to be able not only to fight off withdrawal symptoms but again to experience the 'high'. Thus, a great deal of their suffering is de-addicting against the current of the body's urgent demand, against the pain and violent sickness of withdrawal, so that they can start afresh to feel the 'high'. Knowing that they will have to pay for it by repeating the whole terrible cycle afterwards does not deter them.

Why? If they can break out of the so-called addiction time and time again, why do they re-addict themselves? What *is* the feeling of being high that makes it so irresistible that the mere memory of it causes hundreds of thousands of people to withdraw, re-addict, risk death, steal, prostitute themselves, lose their homes and families and all they have ever cared for or owned?

The fatal attraction of the high, I believe, has not been understood. It has been confused with the very separate demand the drug creates in the body's chemistry, which urges it to continue and increase use once it has upset the chemical balance in its favour. But once the drug is stopped and the last traces of it are gone from the body, the chemical addiction has ceased. There remains only the memory then, the ineradicable memory of the feeling one had.

A twenty-four-year-old addict trying to explain it said this:

Well, the longest I ever stayed clean on the street on my own was when one of my older brothers died of an overdose. I didn't want to use drugs. I think it was like two weeks, three weeks. I thought I would really do it – stay clean – because of my brother. And then one day I was with one of my other brothers and I saw this kid I knew standing on the corner. He was sick. *I* was doing *good*, staying dressed nice, leading a good life. I was happy. He was sick. So I said to him, 'What are you shooting? What's your fix?' And he says, 'Two bags,' so I gave him six dollars. And I know where he's going and what he's going to do, and I know the feeling he's going to get.

It must have hit my mind all the way in the back.

I looked at my brother. He knew what was on my mind and he like shrugged his shoulders, like to say, 'I don't care.' So I said to the kid, 'Look, here's another six dollars. Get two more.' So we got up to the bathroom in some hotel and the kid got off first because he was sick, and my brother got off and then I drew up the stuff, and I just kept sitting around with it in my hand. And I kept thinking about my dead brother. And I didn't want to use, because of what happened to him. Then I says to myself, only it was like to him, 'I hope you'll understand. You know what it's like.'

He felt that his brother would forgive him for not taking his death as seriously as the need for the feeling. The brother had known the feeling himself and therefore would see that there was nothing to do but return to it. The memory of the high hit his mind, as he said, 'all the way in the back'. But what is operating? He can only hint at it. What component of the human mind decides to sacrifice all that must be sacrificed in order to fulfill this one demand?

Another addict put it this way. He said that other people looked for lots of things to make them happy: love, money, power, wives, children, good looks, status, clothes, nice houses, all the rest of it, but all an addict wants is one thing; all his demands can be satisfied at once, by the drug.

This feeling, the high they are talking about, is generally thought to be some bizarre sensation unlike any in a normal person's experience, corresponding to nothing natural and with no understandable relation to the structure of the human personality. It is usually said only that its captives are weak, immature, irresponsible. But that does not explain what constitutes an attraction in the drug so powerful as to overcome all the many other attractions in the civilized world to which a weak person might be susceptible. The life of a heroin addict is not easy, to put it mildly, and to dismiss him as a weakling is not good enough. It remains to understand clearly the difference between a temporarily 'clean' person with a propensity to re-addict and one who has never tried the drug.

An addicted girl who was asked if she ever looked at a 'square' – non-drug-using – girl on the street, interrupted to say, 'And envy her? Yes. Every day. Because she doesn't know what I know. I could never be square like that. I was once, but when I took that first shot, that shattered the whole bit – because then I knew.' But she, too, fails to be explicit and cannot describe, but only refer to, the all-important feeling. 'I knew what it was to be high. I knew what it was to groove with junk. Even the first habit I kicked, which was the *worst* I *ever* kicked, I kicked cold turkey, of my own volition – and I *still* went back to junk.'

This girl was not too weak to go through the terrible business of stopping drug use without any help from an intermediate drug such as methadone, nor was she in jail or in hospital, where the unavailability of the drug might reduce the moment-to-moment strain on her will power. What she could *not* do was to forget what she knew, what she envied the square girl every day of her life for not knowing ... how it feels to be high.

It would be, it seems to me, given the evidence, extremely naïve to assume that those of us who do not know what she knows would behave very differently if we did know. There have been innumerable cases of exactly the same kind of addiction starting with a 'normal' person who has been given morphine in hospital for some painful malady and then remained addicted, reduced to the criminal life of the addict who must support his habit without medical help. Homes and families have not had sufficient value to counteract the mysterious attraction of the drug. The resulting devastation is a matter of record.

Psychiatrists who have made long studies of addicts say that most of them are extremely narcissistic and that their intense preoccupation with heroin is a surface manifestation of a more profound emotional preoccupation with themselves. They show their infantile character in another way as well. They demonstrate immense adult cunning and nerve in the pursuit of heroin, but once they are in possession of their fix, these qualities vanish. They are notoriously clumsy at avoiding arrest – using hiding places of childish obviousness, taking unnecessary risks and invariably blaming their apprehension on someone or something else.

The dominant emotional characteristic of the addict is said to be his enormous compulsion to abdicate responsibility for his own life. One psychiatrist reported that when one of his addict patients saw another patient in an artificial lung, she became enraged, and demanded the lung for herself.*

It appears that, in some very essential way, the feeling heroin gives is like the feeling the infant has in arms. The long, directionless search for a vague something is ended when the heroin user experiences the lost feeling. Once he knows how it can be attained, he cannot keep searching for it in the ways the rest of us do. That is perhaps what the addict meant when she said, '... when I took that first shot, that shattered the whole bit – because then I knew.' The 'whole bit' she is talking about is the motive to find the way to that

* Part I of a two-part series by James Mills in *Life*, 26 February 1965.

feeling the long way, the blind, groping, very indirect way, which in fact does not ever get there, the way we conduct our lives in search of it. The square is spared the immediate awareness of the goal and goes fairly quietly about in the maze of illusions that seem to take him in the right direction, finding his little satisfactions, in a relative way, along the road. But the addict knows where it all is, where it can be got in one place, as the infant gets all he wants in his mother's arms; and he cannot resist returning, guiltily, hounded, ragged and sick, to what in fact it was his birthright to experience. The threat of the horrors surrounding the addict's life, or even of death, is no deterrent in the face of this quintessential need.

If they survive, most addicts *will* stop taking the drug after a number of years, not inconceivably because they have put in enough hours under its influence to have fulfilled the in-arms requirement left over since infancy and are ready at last to move on emotionally to the next set of motives, as a Yequana baby is ready before the age of one. It is hard to account in any other way for the spontaneous cessation of addiction after years of slavery to it, but the fact is that there are almost no elderly users, and it is *not* because they have all died.

Research would soon show if psychotherapy of the sort discussed in the introduction could take the place of drug use. If so, then addicts appear so ill only because the illness we all share has been cruelly brought to the surface in them, their deprivation confronted by fulfilment, albeit a deadly dangerous substitute for its original fulfilment. They may therefore be in more urgent need of treatment, but perhaps it will someday be seen that that is the only difference between them and most of us.

I saw a Sunday evening programme on the television in which there was a heated discussion about morality. There were clergymen and humanist atheists and a young man of the long-haired sort who would like to legalize cannabis as a first priority in improving society. There were a nun and a couple of writers who also held views on how people ought to behave. It occurred to me that in spite of their disagreement and all the emotion invested in their positions, they had a great deal more in common than they had differences. They were all proponents of one strong line or another. They were all idealists in their ways. Some wanted more strictures, more discipline; some wanted more freedom; all of them wanted to better the human condition. They all were seekers, all were if-onlyists, but their ideas of what came after the if-only were widely varied.

It seemed that what we call a moral sense was the continuum sense in a variety of guises. There was a longing for order, an order that would satisfy the needs of the human animal, that would fit without weighing heavily and allow a degree of choice suited to the interests of well-being. It was the 'changed' or 'progressed' society's people trying to think their way through to the kind of stable satisfactoriness that is arrived at through long social evolution by continuum-correct people.

But it appears there are two separate contributors to the feeling of wrongness that is so general in us. One is the individual's sense of the continuum in him acting as a gauge of what is up to its expectations; the other is an even more primordial one.

There is a premise common to every mythology that serenity was once, and at some time again can be, ours.

That we are so universally subject to a conviction that serenity has been lost by us cannot be accounted for solely by the loss, at an early age, of our place in a continuum of appropriate treatment and surroundings. Even people like the relaxed and joyful Yequana, who have not been deprived of their expected experiences, have a mythology that includes a fall from grace, or bliss, and the notion that they live outside that lost state. It also offers the hope of a way back through ritual, custom and a life after death. To describe its particular details would be beside the point. The basic structure, found by cross-cultural anthropology to be quite universal in religious myth, is what is important. It appears that it is enough to be human to require a set of explanations and promises of a certain sort, to fulfil inherent longings.

It would seem that in that enormously long period, running to hundreds of millions of years, before our antecedents developed an intellect able to reflect on troublesome matters like our mortality and purpose, we did indeed live in the only blissful way: entirely in the present. Like every other animal, we enjoyed the great blessing of being incapable of worry. There were discomforts, hungers, wounds, fears and deprivations to be endured even as beasts, but the fall from grace, invariably described as a choice made the wrong way, would have been impossible to creatures without mind enough to make a choice. Only with the advent of the capacity to choose does the fall become possible. And only with choice does the bliss of innocence (the inability to choose wrong) depart. It is not the fact of having chosen wrong but the ability to choose at all that removes innocence. It is not hard to imagine that those aeons of innocence have so impressed themselves upon our most long-standing expectations that there remains a feeling that the serenity that comes with innocence can somehow be had. We enjoyed it in the womb and lost it as we began, in babyhood, to think. It seems so near, yet so far; one can almost recall it. And at moments of enlightenment, or sexual ecstasy, it may even seem to be at hand, graspable, real ... until the awareness of past and future, memories and speculations, reappear to corrupt the pure sense of the present, the simple, perfect sense of being.

In the age-old pursuit of this sense of unalloyed being, this sense of the 'suchness' of things, all things, unconditioned by choices or relativities, men have sought and found disciplines and rituals by which to reverse the tendency to think. Ways have been discovered to still the galloping thoughts of man, put him at peace, leave him not to think but only to be. Awareness has been trained by various means to rest upon emptiness or upon some object or word, chant or exercise. Discomfort and pain have been used to distract the mind from its uneasy coursings, to bring it down to the present, to relieve it of the responsibility of speculation.

Meditation is the word usually given to this procedure of dethinking. It is at the centre of many schools of discipline that seek to raise the serenity level. A commonly used technique is the repetition of a mantra, a word or phrase, as an eraser of thoughts of the associative kind that the mind tends to pursue. As the procession of thoughts is slowed and stopped, the physiological state of the subject changes to resemble, in certain ways, that of an infant. Breathing becomes shallower, and recent experiments have shown that brain waves are produced of a sort that are unlike those of either adult wakefulness or adult sleep.

For those who meditate regularly, there is an apparent increase in serenity, sometimes called spirituality, which lends a stabilizing influence to the rest of their time, time when they are allowing thoughts to manifest themselves unimpeded. It is as though they were, in the case of civilized, in-arms-deprived persons, filling in the gap in infant experience which would have provided greater serenity, by putting themselves into a state like that which was missed, that which possibly is also attained through the use of opiates. The most deprived people, those of our Western cultures, if they meditate, would be putting in a great deal of time moving up to the centredness of a year-old continuum-complete baby. It would take them a vastly greater amount of time to catch up on the missed doses of serenity than people of other cultures whose infancies included a larger proportion of in-arms experience.

For Easterners, who are generally less deprived than the average Westerner, there is a commensurately greater quotient of serenity, so if they take up one of their schools of spiritual discipline – Zen, Yoga, Transcendental Meditation, or whatever – they have much less far to go before they can begin making inroads on the loss of serenity caused by the fall of the human species from animal innocence. The more urgent infantile need comes first, but with time and persistence they do move from one level of peacefulness to another until, in theory, they reach a simple, imperturbable condition that immunizes them to the cares and concerns that go on troubling the rest of us. Wise men, sages or gurus, they are men and women freed from the tyranny of their thought processes; they do not endow the things and events around them with the relative importances that we do.

When I knew them, a large percentage of the Sanema Indians – more than the neighbouring Yequana – were engaged in active cultivation of this extra serenity, or spirituality. Their method includes the occasional use of hallucinogenic drugs, but consists mainly of chanting. The chant, begun with the repetition of a single, short musical phrase of three or four syllables, is continued, like the mantra, in an effortless manner until it commences to elaborate itself with changed or added notes or syllables, with no conscious effort on the part of the chanter. Experienced chanters, like experienced meditators, quickly refind their way to effortlessness each time; the switch from thinking to unthinking is done with ease, but the beginner must guard against effort, against the activities of the intellect, returning to the original phrase whenever the mind interjects some idea that interrupts the completely unguided changes in the chant.

As the Sanema, like the Yequana, are not deprived of their expected experiences in infancy, they have a huge headstart over us on the road to serenity. With a fulfilled personality based solidly in a sense of his own rightness, the Sanema who reproduces the mindless bliss of the infant in himself with frequency and at length can build a freedom from the fringe liabilities of the intellect with far greater speed and effect.

The proportion of Sanema who have attained truly impressive states of joy and harmony with their surroundings is remarkable and would, I am quite certain, be impossible to match anywhere in the West or East. In every clan there are several who live as lightly and happily as the most advanced gurus. I know families in which almost every adult member enjoys these qualities so very rare in civilization.

It became possible in a short time for me to guess, with a fair amount of accuracy, which of a group of Sanema were the shamans from the special looks on their faces, for it is these highly serene persons who customarily have gone in for shamanism.

The connection between the serene state of the cultivated chanter and the powers he may have as a shaman is complicated and mysterious and what little I know of it is not relevant here. What matters is the degree of well-being he attains and why.

Ritual is another form of relief from the burden of choice-making. Speech and action are executed, using the mind and body in a predetermined pattern. The nervous system is busy acting and experiencing, but no thought is required, no choice. One's mental state is very like that of an infant or another species of animal. During the ritual, especially if one has an active part, such as dancing or chanting, the organism is run under a flag far older than that of the intellect. The intellect rests; it stops its everlasting spurring of itself from association to association, from guess to guess, from decision to decision. The rest refreshes not only the intellect but the entire nervous system. It adds a measure of serenity to the balance against the unserenity brought about by thought.

Repetition has long and widely been used to the same end. Whether it is the steady beat of a drum, the monotonous chanting of a rite, a head-lolling, foot-stomping, mind-blowing session at a discotheque or fifty Hail Marys, the effect is 'purifying'. Equanimity is brought forward; anxiety is thrust back. The yearning infant in one is temporarily relieved; the missed experience is that much further filled in, or in those who have only their atavistic nostalgia for innocence to appease, there is that. In all who for a time hand over the reins of the intellect to unthinking being, the cause of greater well-being is served.

6 : Society

Although through childhood and adulthood we become increasingly adaptable to a vast variety of circumstances, there are always limits within which we operate optimally. While to an infant it is largely the caretakers' behaviour that must fulfil his requirements, the growing individual needs more and more the support of his society and its culture to meet his innate expectations. Man can *survive* in appallingly anti-continuum conditions, but his well-being, his joy, his fulfilment as a whole human being, can be lost.

From many points of view he might be better off dead, for the life force, in its ceaseless tending towards repair of damage and completion of developmental phases, among its instruments employs anxiety, pain and an array of other ways of signalling that things are wrong. Unhappiness in all its forms is the result. In civilization, a frequent outcome of the operating of the system is constant misery. Too often, long-unfulfilled needs press from within, while circumstances press from without for which we have inadequate preparation as a species or maturity as an individual. We are living lives for which our evolution did not equip us, and we are also handicapped, in our attempts to cope, by faculties crippled by personal deprivation.

Our standard of living rises without bringing up our standard of well-being, or quality of life, except on rare occasions, usually at the bottom of the socio-economic scale, where such matters as hunger and cold still have reality as factors in the loss of well-being. More often, the causes of unhappiness are less clear-cut.

Possibly the most common cause of loss of an existing level of well-being and the onset of positively unpleasant feelings is apprehension at the ability of the Self to deal with Other. Based on the long-standing sense of having missed something that would have made it right, the Self is weakened at its foundations and falls prey more easily to anxiety over day-to-day reverses. But our expectations also include a *suitable* culture in which to use our faculties, and wherever a person's circumstances fail to remain within the parameters of those expectations, there will be a loss of well-being as he finds he cannot adapt to them.

It is sadly impractical, unrealistic, utopian, to describe a culture to which ours could be changed in order to fill our continuum requirements. Even if the change were made, it would be fairly useless, for unless we were first to become the sort of people to make it work, it would be an unsatisfactory exercise doomed to immediate distortion and eventual disintegration.

Still, it can be of value to try to track down some of the qualities a culture would need to have, in one form or another, if it were to suit the requirements of the continua of its members. For one thing, it would need a language in which the human potential for verbalizing can grow. A child ought to be able to hear adults speaking to one another, and he should have contemporaries with whom to communicate on his own level of interest and development. It is also important that he always have associates slightly older than himself, so that he can have a sense of where he is going before he gets there. This will lend familiarity to the content of his growing interests, so that he can adopt it smoothly when he is ready.

In the same way, the activities of a child need both companionship and example. A society that does not provide them will lose in the efficiency of its members as well as in their sociality.

A sure sign that something is seriously missing in a society is a generation gap. If the younger generation does not take pride in becoming like its elders, then the society has lost its own continuum, its own stability, and probably does not have a culture worth calling one, for it will be in a constant state of change from one unsatisfactory set of values to another. If the younger members of the society feel the older ones are ridiculous, or wrong, or boring, they will have no natural path to follow. They will feel lost, demeaned and cheated and will be angry. The elders, too, will feel cheated and resentful at the loss of continuity in the culture and suffer from a sense of purposelessness along with the young.

The constant promise of a 'better tomorrow' (without which our lives would seem so intolerable that we can scarcely imagine it) is of no interest to the members of an evolved, stable, proud and happy society. Their resistance to change preserves their customs and works to preclude innovation. Our own unsatisfiability, founded in mass deprivation and alienation, on the other hand, overwhelms the cultural expression of our natural tendency to resist change and makes it imperative that we be able to look forward to 'something better' no matter what 'advantages' any of us may now have.

An unchanging way of life is called for that requires the work and cooperation of its members in amounts not excessive to their natures. The work should be of kinds that can be enjoyed by a person whose earlier requirements have been met, so that he has an unimpeded desire to behave socially and to exercise his abilities.

Families should be in close contact with other families, and everyone, during his or her working life, ought to have the opportunity for companionship and cooperation. A woman left alone every day with her children is deprived of social stimulation and needs emotional and intellectual support they cannot give. The result is bad for mother, child, family and society.

In our own society housewives, instead of playing long-suffering wife to a house, might arrange to do their housework with nearby friends, perhaps working together first in one house and then in another. What are now called playgroups afford all the ingredients for a successful working group, where the mothers, and other people as well, could be engaged in useful and interesting work while the children invent their own games or join in the work without any more adult attention than is absolutely necessary to allow them to participate. The children's place on the periphery, rather than at the centre, of adult concern will permit them to find their own interests and pace without pressure, always providing there is enough variety of materials and scope in the area for exercising and discovering their potential. But whether the main activity is weaving, manufacturing a product, painting, sculpting, mending or whatever, it should be done primarily by and for the grown-ups and the children allowed to join in without unduly disrupting it. In this way, everyone will be behaving in a natural, unforced way, with no strain on the parents' part to confine their minds to a childish level or upon the children to try to adapt themselves to what an adult believes is best for them, thus preventing their own initiative from motivating them smoothly and without conflict.

Children ought to be able to accompany adults almost wherever they go. In cultures like ours, where this is now largely impossible, schools and teachers might learn to take fuller advantage of the tendencies of children to imitate and practise skills on their own initiative rather than have them 'taught'.

In a continuum-correct society the generations would live under the same roof, to the advantage of all. Grandparents would help as much as they could, and people at the height of their working powers would not begrudge support to their elders any more than to their children. But again, the truly enriching cohabitation of the generations depends upon their having fulfilled personalities and not pulling, as most of us would, at one another's emotions to satisfy leftover infantile needs for attention and care.

Leadership would emerge naturally among the members of a society, very much as it does among children, and confine itself to taking initiatives only when individual ones are impractical. The followers should be the ones to decide whom they will follow and should be free to change leaders as suits their convenience. In a continuum culture like that of the Yequana, the functioning of leaders is minimal, and it is possible for any individual to decide not to act on the leader's decision if he prefers; but it will be a long time before *we* can live so close to anarchy with success. It is none the less worth while keeping in mind as a direction in which to move when and if our cultures and population pressures permit.

The number of people who live and work together would vary from a few families to several hundred people, so that the individual would be interested in maintaining good relations with all the people with whom he deals. The knowledge that one will continue to associate with the same people is a strong motive to treat them fairly, and with respect, even in our own world, where a fixed group of neighbours, as in country communities or small villages, find themselves thrown together as a society. The human animal cannot really live with thousands or millions of others. He can have relationships with a limited number only, and in large cities it can be seen that among the throngs, each person has a more or less tribe-sized circle of work and social associates. The others around him, however, have the effect of making him feel that there are an infinite number of chances for new relationships if the old ones are allowed to fail.

The Yequana taught me far more refined ways of dealing with people than the ones I had known in civilization. Their way of greeting visitors struck me as particularly sound.

I saw it first when I arrived in a Yequana village with two Yequana travellers from a distant village. I was not then expected to know how to behave, so Wenito, the old fellow who had been among Venezuelans in his youth and knew some Spanish came and greeted me with the customary Venezuelan pat on the shoulder and after some conversation showed me where to put my hammock.

But my two companions received very different treatment. They seated themselves not far away from me under the great round roof without a word to or from anyone, and they did not look at, or speak to, one another. The residents came and went at various distances in the course of their normal business, but none gave so much as a glance at the visitors. For about an hour and a half the two men sat motionless and silent; then a woman came quietly and placed some food on the ground before them and walked away. The men did not reach immediately for the food but after a moment ate some in silence. Then the bowls were taken quietly away and more time elapsed.

Eventually, a man approached in a leisurely way and stood leaning against one of the roof poles behind the visitors. After several moments he spoke, very softly, a few syllables. Easily two minutes passed before the elder visitor answered, also briefly. Again the silence closed over them. When they spoke again it was as though each utterance was referred back to the reigning silence out of which it had come. The personal peace and dignity of each man suffered no imposition. As the exchange became more lively, others came, stood awhile, then joined in. They all seemed to have a sense of the serenity of each man, which had to be preserved. No one interrupted anyone else; emotional pressure was absent from any voice. Every man remained balanced on his own centre.

It was not long before laughter blossomed among the talk, bringing the dozen or so men into rising and falling waves of unison between their speeches.

At sunset the women served a meal to the assembled men; by now every one in the village. News was exchanged, and there was a great deal of laughter. Both residents and visitors were perfectly assimilated in the atmosphere without having had recourse to falseness or nervousness. The silences had not been a sign of the breakdown of communication but a time for each man to be at peace with himself and to be assured that the others were the same.

When the men of the village went on long trips to trade with other Indians, they were received, on their return, with the same procedure by their families and clansmen: left to sit in silence long enough to recapture the feel of village life, then casually approached without pressure or demanding demonstrations of emotion.

One tends to view foreign or exotic peoples as having fairly uniform personalities, and primitives perhaps even more. But, of course, this is not the case. Conformity to the local mores gives a certain similarity to the behaviour of the members of a society, but differences among individuals are, in the more continuum-correct society, freer expressions of innate characteristics, since the society has no need to fear or try to suppress them.

In civilized societies, on the other hand, in varying degrees according to their departure from continuum standards, the differences among people are largely expressions of the ways in which they have adapted to the distortions in their personalities caused by the qualities and quantities of deprivation they have experienced. They are often, therefore, antisocial, and the society comes to fear them and, with them, all other signs of nonconformity in its members. The more anti-continuum the culture, in general, the more pressure is likely to be brought to bear upon the individual to present a façade of conformity to a norm in his public and private conduct.

I was once astonished to see a Yequana take it into his head to climb to the top of the hill overlooking the village to pound a drum and shout at the top of his lungs for a good half-hour before his impulse was satisfied. He felt like doing it for reasons of his own and did it without any apparent concern for what the neighbours would think, though it was not a 'done thing'. My own surprise was because I had never questioned my society's unwritten law that sane members of the community inhibit their odd or 'irrational' impulses in order to avoid being feared or mistrusted.

As a corollary of this rule in our culture, the most celebrated, accepted persons among us – film stars, pop stars, figures like Winston Churchill, Albert Einstein and Gandhi – have a licence to dress and behave in far less conforming ways than they could have permitted themselves before they became well enough known to be above suspicion. Even the tragic aberrations of a Judy Garland were somehow not as frightening to the public as the same sort of behaviour would have been in a neighbour, for she was a celebrity, approved by millions of others, so there was no fear in accepting whatever she did. One did not have to rely upon one's own doubtful ability to judge and accept.

It is pretty readily observable that the less reliable among us are the more suspicious of others. This can be regarded as neurotic and antisocial in a society that prescribes that its members be reliable, but it can also be a perfectly social attitude in a society in which it is the custom to try to cheat the other fellow whenever possible, assuming, of course, that he will be doing the same. One is then relying upon the members of one's culture to be unreliable and is keeping a constant lookout for a chance to beat them at the game. It works as a *modus vivendi* in many countries, only perhaps being a bit hard on the unsuspecting visitor from a country where fair play is an important part of what is considered social behaviour.

The Yequana view of business dealings seemed to me to be based, like their manner of receiving new arrivals, on a supreme desire not to create tension. I had a rare chance of further insight into the extent of their gentlemanliness when I had business to transact with Anchu, the Yequana chief. It was when he had initiated the campaign to guide me to behave as they do, instead of treating me in the usual way as a non-human, not to be given the respect due a real person (a Yequana) nor expected to behave like one. None of the lessons he gave me were verbal instructions or explanations but experiences that tended to bring out in me, or rather to disconfuse, my innate ability to recognize and to prefer what was best suited to the circumstances. He was, one could say, trying to disengage my continuum sense from the innumerable interferences my own culture had imposed upon it.

It was the occasion I mentioned earlier on which Anchu had asked me what I would take in exchange for a piece of Venetian glass costume jewellery. I immediately said I wanted sugar cane, as our expedition had lost its supply of sugar when a canoe overturned in a rapids, and my craving for anything sweet had begun to resemble an obsession. We went the next day to the cane field with his wife (among the Yequana, only women cut sugar cane) to complete the transaction.

Anchu and I sat on a log beside the field while the woman went in and came out with four stalks. She dropped them to the ground and Anchu asked me if I wanted more.

Of course I wanted more; I wanted as much as I could get, so I said yes.

The wife went back and returned with two more stalks. She put them with the others.

'More?' Anchu asked me.

And again I said, 'Yes, more!' But then the light dawned. We were not bargaining in the every-man-for-himself way I had assumed. Anchu was asking me to judge in a comradely and trusting way what would be a fair exchange and was willing to abide by my evaluation. When I realized my mistake I was embarrassed and called out after his wife, who had gone back for the fourth time into the field with her machete, 'Toini!' ('Only one!') So the bargain was made for seven stalks, and the bargaining had contained no setting of one against the other in any way, nor any tension in either of us (after I had understood).

I do not think there is much likelihood of our trading techniques becoming as 'civilized' as Yequana ones. I offer the story only as an example of what can become accepted as a way to operate if the culture prescribes it and the members of the society can be counted upon to be social rather than antisocial in their motivations.

A society that prescribes less pleasant and less attractive customs will still elicit conformity from socially motivated members. The Sanema Indians, whose culture differs enormously from that of the Yequana, for example, consider it right to raid the village of another

Sanema clan and steal as many young women and kill as many men as possible.

When and why this part of their culture came into being, or why the Jivaro Indians on the other side of the South American continent have it that every death must be avenged whatever its cause, one does not know. What is useful to observe is that a society of socially motivated individuals will live by the dictates of its culture and can be relied upon to do so. The antisocial, or criminal, character does not develop in people whose continuum expectations have not been disappointed. Just as a back-street murderer commits an antisocial act and a soldier killing an enemy does not, it is the motive, not the act, that counts in measuring the sociality of the perpetrator.

We presumably would like it to be a humane culture to which our society subscribes its cooperative inclinations. But to say 'humane' must also imply respect for the human continuum. A culture that requires people to live in a way for which their evolution has not prepared them, that does not fulfil their innate expectations and therefore pushes their adaptability beyond its limits, is bound to damage their personalities.

One way of pushing the human personality too far is by depriving it of its minimum requirement for variety of stimuli. The resulting loss of well-being takes a form called boredom. The continuum sense, by producing this unpleasant feeling, motivates the person to change what he is doing. We in civilization do not customarily feel we have a 'right' not to be bored, and so we spend years doing monotonous work in factories and offices or alone all day doing uninteresting chores.

The Yequana, on the other hand, with their quick, sharp sense of the limits of their own continua, of their capacity for adaptation without loss of well-being, heed immediately the call to stop what they are doing when boredom threatens.

They have found ways of getting around the menace of boredom when they want to do a job entailing monotonous work. For one thing, women who want many straight rows of sharp metal bits hammered into a board for grating manioc, instead of putting in row after monotonous row, introduce the points in a diamond pattern first, then fill in all the spaces later, so that the pattern disappears, its purpose, to entertain the artisan, having been served.

Another example is roof-building, done by lashing each palm leaf to a framework with a liana. The men are seated on a scaffold with piles of leaves and inch along, securing them one by one. They have various means of escaping boredom while still getting a large roof made. For one thing, they invite all the men from their own and any nearby village to help the job go quickly. Before they arrive, the women have fermented enough manioc to keep everyone more or less tipsy during the days the work requires, thereby narrowing awareness and with it the normal susceptibility to boredom. To add to the festive atmosphere, beads, feathers and paint are worn, and someone is marching about beating a drum most of the time. The men and boys talk and joke while at work and keep at it only until they feel like coming down to do something else as a change. Sometimes a large number are working at once and sometimes only a few are in the mood. It works admirably for everyone; all the guests are fed by the families whose house it will be and who have done some intensive hunting beforehand to provide meat.

During the days of drinking, when everyone is somewhat intoxicated, and the nights when men, women, and children are drinking even more, and the men are very drunk, it is impressive to note again that there is no sign of aggressiveness.

It is perhaps also an expression of their fulfilled personalities that they feel so little need to make judgements upon one another and can so easily accept individual differences. It is observable among us as well that the more frustrated, the more alienated, people are, the more they feel they must judge and distinguish between others as acceptable or unacceptable either on a personal basis or in groups, as in religious, political, national, racial, sexual or even age conflict.

Self-hate, resulting from not having been given the sense of one's own rightness in infancy, is, of course, a major basis for irrational hatred of others.

It is interesting that although the Yequana regard the Sanema Indians as inferior beings with barbaric ways, and the Sanema harbour a mild resentment of the Yequana's haughty treatment of them, neither group has the slightest wish to hurt or interfere with the other's way of life. They visit and trade with one another often and make jokes behind one another's back, but there is no conflict between them ever.

A great part of our tragedy is that we have lost the sense of our 'rights' as members of the human species. Not only do we accept boredom with resignation, but innumerable other infringements of what is left of our continuum after the ravages of infancy and childhood. We say, for example, 'It is cruel to keep so large an animal in a flat in town,' but we are speaking of dogs, never of people, who are even larger and more sensitive to their surroundings. We permit ourselves to be bombarded with noise from machinery, traffic and other people's radios and expect to be treated rudely by strangers. We are learning to expect to be despised by our children and to be irritated by our parents. We accept living with gnawing insecurities not only about our own ability at work and socially but also very often about our marriages. We take it for granted that life is hard and feel *lucky* to have whatever happiness we get. We do not look upon happiness as a birthright, nor do we expect it to be more than peace or contentment. Real joy, the state in which the Yequana spend much of their lives, is exceedingly rare among us.

If we had the opportunity to live the sort of life for which we have evolved, a great many of our present motives would be affected. For one thing, we would not imagine that children must be happier than adults, nor that the young adult must be happier than the old. As we have seen, we hold this view largely because we are in constant pursuit of some goal that we hope will restore our lost sense of rightness about our lives. As we attain the goals and find ourselves still missing that nameless something kept from us since infancy, we lose by degrees our belief that the next set of hopes will relieve our persistent longings. We also teach ourselves to accept 'reality' or ease the pain of repeated disappointment as best we can. At a certain point in mid-life we begin to tell ourselves that we have missed, for one reason or another, the chance to enjoy complete well-being and must live with the consequences in a state of permanent compromise. This state of affairs is hardly conducive to joy.

Living as one has evolved to do, one's history is very different. Babyhood desires give way to those of the successive phases of childhood and each fulfilled set of desires gives way to the next. The desire to play games fades away; the desire to work becomes increasingly strong as one becomes an adult; the desire to find and share life with an attractive member of the opposite sex, fulfilled, gives rise to a desire to work for the mate and to have children together. Maternal and paternal motives develop towards the children. The need to associate with one's similars is fulfilled from childhood to death. As the needs of adults in their prime to initiate and carry through their projects become fulfilled and age begins to reduce physical powers, desires are for seeing one's loved ones succeed, for peace, for less variety in experiences, to feel that things are moving through the cycle of life with less help from oneself and ultimately, with no help, as the last of life's succession of desires is fulfilled and is replaced by none but the wish to rest, to know no more, to cease.

In every phase, founded firmly upon the completion of the preceding ones, the stimulus of desire receives its full response. There is, therefore, no genuine advantage in being young over being old. Each time has its particular joys, and after one has relinquished each set of desires as it runs its course, there can be no cause to envy the young nor to wish for any age other than one's own and the pleasures it brings with it, up to and including death.

Pain and illness, the deaths of those one loves, discomforts and disappointments mar the happy norm, but they do not alter the fact that happiness *is* the norm or affect the tendency of the continuum to restore it, to heal it, after any disturbance.

The point is that the continuum sense, allowed to function throughout our lives, is capable of looking after our interests better than any intellectually devised system could begin to do.

In the infant kept in constant contact with the body of a caretaker, his energy field becomes one with hers and excess energy can be discharged for both of them by her activities alone. The infant can remain relaxed, free of accumulating tension, as his extra energy flows into hers.

There is a remarkable contrast between the behaviour of Yequana infants in arms and our own infants, most of whose time is spent in physical isolation. The Yequana babies are soft and easy to handle, unresistant to being held or carried in any convenient position. Our infants, on the other hand, kick their legs out straight, wave their arms violently and stiffen their backs into strained arches. They wriggle and strain in their cots and prams and are difficult to hold if they go through the same motions when we pick them up. They are trying to relieve the mounting tension caused by having taken in more energy than they can comfortably contain or discharge. They often emit piercing screams when excited by the attention of some person, as well as squirming. Although they are expressing pleasure, the stimulus causes a violent muscular reaction that expends some of the pent-up energy.

The passive infant, snug inside his continuum, his expectations for continual physical contact met, makes little contribution towards the discharge of energy, leaving it to the active adult or child who is carrying him. But this situation is radically changed the moment the baby has completed the in-arms phase and begins to crawl. The cycling of his own energy must then be done by himself. There is an enormous increase in his activity. In a short time the crawling becomes efficient and he travels at impressive speeds, which are greatly accelerated when he begins to creep. If he is not restricted, he then creeps energetically and persistently over the available area, using up his excess energy as he explores the world he will live in.

When he starts to walk and run and to play, he does so at a pace which, in an adult, would appear quite frenzied. An adult trying to keep up with him would soon be exhausted. His contemporaries and older children are more suitable companions for him. He wants to imitate them, and he does so to the best of his ever-increasing ability. No one limits his terrific activity but himself. When he tires he goes to his mother to rest or, when he is older, to his bed.

But a child is unable to discharge enough energy to remain comfortable if for some reason, as so often happens in civilized situations, his actions are limited by insufficient time or space in which to play or being imprisoned in a playpen, harness, cot, or high-chair.

When he passes the stage at which he kicks and waves and stiffens to relieve the discomfort of unexpressed energy, he is soon likely to discover that the uncomfortable excess is concentrated in his genitals to a large extent and that by stimulating them further he can cause the excess energy in the rest of his body to flow into them until they build up pressure enough to bring about release. In this way, masturbation becomes a safety valve for excess energy not consumed in a child's daily activities.

In adulthood, excess energy is similarly concentrated by sexual foreplay and released by orgasm. Thus the sexual act serves two distinct purposes, the one reproductive, the other as restorer of a comfortable energy level.

In people whose deprivations have left them to maintain a state of tension among the inharmonious aspects of their personalities, orgasm often releases only a superficial part of the energy tied up in their permanently tensed muscles. This incomplete release of the excess energy creates a fairly chronic state of dissastisfaction, which manifests itself in bad temper, an inordinate interest in sex, inability to concentrate, nervousness, promiscuity.

To make matters worse for the deprived adult, his or her need for the physical expression of sex is mixed with the need left over from infancy for non-sexual physical contact. In general, this latter need is not recognized in our society, and any wish for contact is construed as sexual. So the taboos against sex are also applied to all the comforting non-sexual forms of physical contact.

Even the children and adults of the Yequana, who have all the required contact in infancy, still enjoy a great deal of contact, sitting close together, resting in the same hammock or grooming one another.

Far more than they do *we* need to break through the present taboo and take cognizance of the human need for the reassurance of contact. Our unfulfilled infantile need adds immeasurably to the requirement we would naturally have for it as children and adults. But as the need continues, so does the chance to fill it, if only we will.

Under the broad banner of sex, undistinguished from it as a separate impulse is the need to be held, surrounded by the protection of another person, to be babied and made to feel lovable not because one has brought home a salary or baked a cake, but simply because one exists. The reassuring atmosphere created by baby talk and the use of baby names ('Bunnykins', 'Daddy's little girl') between marriage partners helps to allow them to fill in the experiential gaps left by their parents' neglect. The widespread use of baby talk is in itself a testimony to the continuing nature of the need.

Often the desire for sex and the desire for affection lead from one to the other. In adults the satisfaction of the one pressing need may leave the other to arise. A day at the office that has produced particular insecurity may cause a husband to want to hold and be held by his wife and to be treated with affection; but when that requirement is met he may find that his interest in her turns to a sexual one. But in our society he may feel *obliged* to go on to sex, since the two needs are not distinct in his mind as independent of one another.

Adult love among the in-arms-deprived is, perforce, an admixture of the two needs, which varies from person to person with the nature of the deprivation. Couples must learn to take into account their own and their mate's special requirements and try to cater for them as best they can if the marriage is to be a 'good' one.

But the confusion between the need for sex and the need for affection, a maternal kind of physical contact, the confusion that gives rise to phrases like 'red-hot mama', is important to resolve. I believe that with a clear notion of the distinction and a little practice in dissociating the two, a great deal more affection could be exchanged without the complications of sexual involvement when it is not wanted. The vast reservoir of longing for physical comforting might be significantly reduced if it became socially acceptable to hold hands with a walking companion of either sex, to sit touching, not just near, talking companions, to sit on people's laps in public as well as in private, to stroke a tempting head of hair when the mood takes one, to hug more freely and more publicly, and in general not to curb one's affectionate impulses unless they would be unwelcome.

Moves have been made in the direction of more contact in recent years, and hugs have become acceptable, not only among Latins and members of the theatrical professions, but increasingly in other sectors of society, first between women and women and women and men, then, finally between men and men.

Starting from the continuum point of view, understanding what it is that humans need and why we need it, it is possible to comprehend our own behaviour and that of others more usefully. We might stop blaming our parents or society for wronging us and understand that we are all victims of deprivation. Archbishops and hippies, artists and scientists, schoolteachers and naughty little boys – all are trying to find the way to a sense of rightness. So are film stars, politicians, criminals, comedians, homosexuals, women's liberationists, clergymen and businessmen. Being the animals we are, we cannot but grope towards fulfilling our expectations, no matter how irrational a tangle our combinations of deprivations make of our actual behaviour.

But understanding what is the trouble and realizing that we are all merely victims of victims, that no one is winning, will not cure us. At best it may help us to choose a step in the right direction rather than a further step away from well-being.

Small children, deprived in infancy, benefit enormously from simply being welcomed on a parent's (or anyone's) lap at every possible opportunity and being expected to sleep in their parents' bed with them. It is not long before they have all they require and want a bed of their own, just as they would have done earlier had they shared their parents' bed from birth.

At this moment in history, with our customs as they are, sleeping with one's baby seems a wildly radical thing to advocate. And so, of course, does carrying him around or having him held by someone, at every moment, asleep or awake. *But in the light of the continuum and its millions of years, it is only our tiny history that appears radical in its departures from the long-established norms of human and pre-human experience.*

There are women and men who protest that they would be afraid of rolling over on a sleeping infant or of smothering him under the bedclothes. But a person asleep is neither dead nor in a coma unless dead drunk, heavily drugged or extremely ill. Without waking up, one has a degree of constant awareness.

I remember the first nights I shared my bed with a two-pound baby woolly monkey. I awoke a dozen times the first night in fear of squashing her. The second night was almost as bad, but within a few days I had learned that I was aware of her position while I slept, and slept taking her into account, like many another big animal sleeping with a small one. The chances of a baby being smothered in his parents' bedcovers seem to me less, if anything, given their awareness of him, than the chances under his own covers, alone in his room.

There is concern, too, about the infant being present when his parents make love. Among the Yequana, his presence is taken as a matter of course, and must have been so as well during the hundreds of millennia before us.

It may even be that in *not* being present he is missing an important psycho-biological link with his parents, which leaves him with a sense of longing for it that turns later into a repressed, guilt-laden Oedipus (or Electra) wish to make love to the parent of the opposite sex, when in fact he really wanted the infant's passive role in the first place and translated the longing into one for active participation when the quality of his sexuality changed and passive participation could no longer be remembered or imagined. Research might show that we can preclude this powerful source of discomfiting, antisocial-izing guilt.

A very widely held view is that giving a baby or child too much attention will prevent him from becoming independent and that carrying him about full-time will weaken his self-reliance. We have already seen that self-reliance itself comes from a completed in-arms phase, but it is one in which the infant is always present but *rarely the centre of attention*. He is simply there, in the midst of his caretaker's life, constantly experiencing things, safely being held. When he leaves his mother's knee and begins to crawl, creep and walk about in the world beyond her body, he does so without interference ('protection'). His mother's role then is to be *available* when he comes to or calls for her. It is not for her to direct his activities, nor to protect him from dangers from which he would be fully capable of protecting himself if given the chance. This is perhaps the most difficult part of switching to continuum ways. Each mother will have to trust her baby's capacity for self-preservation as far as she is able. Few could manage to allow the free playing with sharp knives and fire and the freedom of watersides that the Yequana permit without a thought, knowing the enormous self-protective talents of babies as they do; but the less the civilized mother takes over responsibility for her baby's safety, the sooner and better he will become independent. He will know when he needs help or comfort. He should be left to be the initiator. He should never be kept from his mother, but she ought to *offer* the absolute minimum of guidance to him.

The overprotected, weakened child is the one whose initiative has been constantly usurped by an over-eager mother. It is not the child who was held in arms during the first important months when he required it.

There will, of course, be difficulty in translating the lessons learned about the continuum from the Yequana so that they can improve matters in our own very different circumstances in civilization. I believe that making up one's mind to stay as close to the continuum as possible is itself the most useful step. Discovering ways to do so, once the will is there, is largely a matter of using one's common sense.

Once a mother realizes that seeing that her baby is carried about for the first six or eight months will ensure his self-reliance and lay the foundations for his becoming social, undemanding and positively helpful for the next fifteen or twenty years he will be at home, even her self-interest will tell her not to spare herself the 'trouble' of carrying him while she is doing her housework or shopping.

I believe that the vast majority of parents truly love their children and deprive them of the experiences so essential to their happiness only because they have no idea what they are causing them to suffer. If they understood the agony of the baby left to weep in his cot, his terrible longing and the consequences of the suffering, the effects of the deprivation upon his personality's development and potential for making a satisfactory life, I do not doubt that they would fight to prevent his being left alone for a minute.

I further believe that once a mother begins to serve her baby's continuum (and thus her own as a mother), the culturally confused instinct in her will reassert itself and reconnect her natural motives. She will not *want* to put her baby down. When he cries, the signal will go directly to her heart, unbaffled by any schools of thought on child-rearing. If she goes through the correct motions at first, I am sure the ancient instinct will soon take over; for the continuum is a powerful force and never ceases to try to reinstate itself. The sense of rightness felt by the mother when she is behaving in accordance with nature will do far more to re-establish the continuum in her than anything this book may have conveyed to her as theory.*

The difference between our way of life and that of the Yequana is irrelevant to the principles of human nature we are considering.

Many mothers have jobs to which they would not be permitted to bring their babies. But very often these jobs are a matter of choice; the mothers could, if they realized the urgency of their presence during the baby's first year, give up the job in order to avert the deprivations which would damage the baby's entire life and be a burden to her for years as well.

On the other hand, there are mothers who must work. But they do not leave their children at home alone; they hire someone to look after them or leave them with a grandmother or make some other arrangement for the children to be accompanied. Whichever is the case, the caretaker can be instructed to carry the baby with her. Babysitters, hired for an evening, can be asked to sit the baby, not just the television set. They can hold the baby on their laps as they watch the television or do their homework. The noise and light will not disturb or harm him, but being left alone will.

Holding a baby while doing housework is a matter of practice. A sling over one shoulder that supports the baby on the opposite hip

---

*This has, since I first wrote it, been borne out by many Western mothers. Though several thought they would never go so far as to maintain constant, twenty-four-hour-a-day contact, they found that the more they carried their babies, the more they wanted to. Their instincts did, indeed, take over (see introduction).

is helpful. Dusting and vacuum cleaning can be done mainly with one hand. Bed making will be a little more difficult, but a resourceful mother will find a way to do it. Cooking is largely a matter of keeping one's body between the cooker and the baby when there is danger of splashing. The problem of shopping is mostly one of having a capacious shopping bag and not buying more than one can carry at once. It would not be a bad idea, as long as there are so many prams in the world, to put the shopping in them and carry the baby. There are also back carriers for babies that have straps over both the adult's shoulders and leave her hands free. Front carriers cut out much important experience, for the baby can only strain uncomfortably, trying to see what is going on behind its back, and the mother's freedom is also unnecessarily restricted after the first weeks. For most circumstances, the hip position is best.

It would help immeasurably if we could see baby care as a non-activity. We should learn to regard it as nothing to do. Working, shopping, cooking, cleaning, walking and talking with friends are things to do, to make time for, to think of as activities. The baby (with other children) is simply brought along as a matter of course; no special time need be set aside for him, apart from the minutes devoted to changing nappies. His bath can be part of his mother's. Breast-feeding need not stop all other activity either. It is only a matter of changing one's baby-centred thought patterns to those more suitable for a capable, intelligent being whose nature it is to enjoy work and the companionship of other adults.

There are endless obstacles to the human continuum in our present way of life. Not only do we have anti-continuum customs like separating infants from their mothers at birth in hospitals, using prams and cots and playpens, and not expecting a new mother to bring her baby along on social engagements, but our dwellings are cut off from one another, so mothers are deprived of the company of their contemporaries and suffer from boredom, and the children do not have free and easy access to their contemporaries and older children, except in some playgroups and schools. Even there, they usually are fairly confined to children of exactly their own age, and the teachers too often instruct the children in what to do instead of setting examples that the children would naturally follow.

Still, there are parks where parents and children can meet and age groups are not separated. But there will be handicaps to every parent and child, imposed, if by nothing else, by the past, the way the parents were brought up and the longstanding notions about how to rear children that are part of our culture. There will be the usual fear of not conforming with the going customs, for the continuum itself makes us tend to conform to whatever our society does.

A child will not be able to follow his father to his office, and unless the father is someone like a farmer, the child will have to seek examples elsewhere.

People whose job it will be to assume the role of example setters, who will demonstrate the skills of our society, will be the ones children can follow. If these educators base their relationship with children upon *being available* to watch, follow and assist, children will be able to utilize their own efficient, natural way of educating themselves by making use of the people, things and events of their world to imitate, observe and practise upon, motivated by their own social, imitative natures. Older children can be expected to show younger ones how things are done. It is natural for them to do so and far less strain on everyone concerned. It is also excellent practice for the 'teaching' children to be used in this way by their juniors. There can be no more effective way to educate.

Another obstacle to the continuum in our way of life is our view that we own our children and consequently have the right to treat them any way we choose, short of battering or killing them. They have no legal right not to be tortured by longing for their mothers and left to scream their agony unheeded. The fact that they are human and capable of suffering does not in itself give them any legal rights, as it does adults made to suffer cruelties by other adults. The fact that their torment in infancy also prejudices their ability to enjoy the rest of their lives and is, therefore, an immeasurable injury done them, does not help their legal position.

Babies cannot articulate complaints. They cannot go to an authority and protest. They cannot even connect the agony they have endured with its cause; they are happy to see their mother when she at last arrives.

In our society rights are granted not because one suffers injury but because one complains of it. Only the most rudimentary rights are accorded to animals, and in very few countries. Likewise, indigenous primitives, who have no medium through which to complain, are given few of the rights their conquerors grant one another.

Custom has left the treatment of infants to maternal discretion. But should every mother be free to neglect her child, to slap him for crying, to feed him when she wants, not when he wants, to leave him suffering alone in a room for hours, days, months, when it is his very nature to be in the midst of life?

The societies for the prevention of cruelty to babies and children concern themselves only with the grossest sort of abuse. Our society must be helped to see the gravity of the crime against infants that is today considered normal treatment.

Even in a culture like ours, developed without taking the real needs of its people into account, with an understanding of the human continuum, there is room to improve our chances and reduce our errors in every small way that presents itself from day to day.

Without waiting to change society at all, we can behave correctly towards our infants and give them a sound personal base from which to deal with whatever situations they meet. Instead of depriving them so that they have only one hand with which to cope with the outside world, while the other is busy with inner conflicts, we can set them on their feet with both hands ready to take on outside challenges.

Once we fully recognize the consequences of our treatment of babies, children, one another and ourselves, and learn to respect the real character of our species, we cannot fail to discover a great deal more of our potential for joy.

The Liedloff Continuum Network
c/o Stella Barclay,
62 Linkside,
London N12 7LG,
England

The Liedloff Continuum Network is a world network of people interested in making the Continuum Concept part of their lives.

If you would like to know the names of network members near you, please write to the above address. Please say whether you would like your name to be included on the list. There is also a network newsletter. If you would like to receive information about this and/or the list, please send a stamped, self-addressed envelope.

Index

imitation, 90–3
imprinting, 69–70
impulses, leftover, 77
incubators, 82
independence development, 80, 82, 88–
  93, 105–6, 121, 154–5
Indians, North American
  vertigo, lack of, 28, 68
Indians, South American
  hearing development, 54
  vertigo, lack of, 68
  see also named tribes
individuality, respect for, 97–8, 100,
  103
infantile needs, 116
infantilism, 127, 131, 132
infants, *see* babies *and* child care
innate ability, *see* instinct
innate tendencies, 95
innocence, 133–4, 137
insanity, 60, 81
instinct
  child rearing, 155–6
  deprivation, effect of, 60
  mothers, 124
  opportunities to reinstate, 37
  strength of, 87
  undermining, 34–5
  see also behaviour
intellect
  contradiction of evolved nature, 93–
    94
  development, 44
  memory development, 56–7
  replacing instinct, 34–5, 78–9
  role of, 56
  theories of infant care, 34–5, 48–9,
    82, 156
  thought processes, 133–4, 135, 136

Jivaro Indians, 146
joy, *see* happiness
jungle
  ecosystems, 24
  expeditions
    first, 19–27
    second, 27–31, 33, 98
    third, 32, 33, 99–100
    fourth, 32, 33, 94, 101
    fifth, 32–3
  fascination of, 22–3

hazards, 108
reason for joining, 19

Kamala, the wolf child, 52, 53
Katawehu, Yequana boy, 106
Kempe, Prof. C. Henry, 124

labour-saving, 119
Lake, Dr Frank, 17
language, *see* speech
laughter, 112
leadership, 141
learning
  by imitation, 90–3, 140–1, 152,
    157–8
  cultural awareness, 52–3, 90–3
  development, 60
  interplay with instinct, 87–8
  process, 39
  selective 52–3
  'unlearning', 28, 32
legal position of children, 158
lesbianism, 126
life force, 138
Loeb Center for Nursing and Rehabilitation, 127–8
London Hospital for Sick Children, 124–
  25
loneliness, 57, 81, 112
Lorenz, Konrad, 69
lost children, 94–5
lovability, 116, 117, 121–2, 152
love objects, 117

magical powers, 55–6
mantra, 134, 135
marriage, 116–17, 121, 148–9, 152
Martin, Helen L., 124–5
martyrs, 122
Masawiu, Yequana Indian, 101–2
masturbation, 151
materialism, 114–15, 121, 130, 145
maternal role *see* mothering
maturity, 44
mechanisms
  editing, 54–5
  stabilizing, 36, 57–61, 93–4
  survival, 89–90
meditation, 134–6
memory, 42, 56–7
mental health, 81

FOR THE BEST IN PAPERBACKS, LOOK FOR THE

In every corner of the world, on every subject under the sun, Penguin represents quality and variety – the very best in publishing today.

For complete information about books available from Penguin – including Puffins, Penguin Classics and Arkana – and how to order them, write to us at the appropriate address below. Please note that for copyright reasons the selection of books varies from country to country.

In the United Kingdom: Please write to *Dept E.P., Penguin Books Ltd, Harmondsworth, Middlesex, UB7 0DA.*

If you have any difficulty in obtaining a title, please send your order with the correct money, plus ten per cent for postage and packaging, to *PO Box No 11, West Drayton, Middlesex*

In the United States: Please write to *Dept BA, Penguin, 299 Murray Hill Parkway, East Rutherford, New Jersey 07073*

In Canada: Please write to *Penguin Books Canada Ltd, 2801 John Street, Markham, Ontario L3R 1B4*

In Australia: Please write to the *Marketing Department, Penguin Books Australia Ltd, P.O. Box 257, Ringwood, Victoria 3134*

In New Zealand: Please write to the *Marketing Department, Penguin Books (NZ) Ltd, Private Bag, Takapuna, Auckland 9*

In India: Please write to *Penguin Overseas Ltd, 706 Eros Apartments, 56 Nehru Place, New Delhi, 110019*

In the Netherlands: Please write to *Penguin Books Netherlands B.V., Postbus 195, NL–1380AD Weesp*

In West Germany: Please write to *Penguin Books Ltd, Friedrichstrasse 10–12, D–6000 Frankfurt/Main 1*

In Spain: Please write to *Longman Penguin España, Calle San Nicolas 15, E–28013 Madrid*

In Italy: Please write to *Penguin Italia s.r.l., Via Como 4, I-20096 Pioltello (Milano)*

In France: Please write to *Penguin Books Ltd, 39 Rue de Montmorency, F-75003 Paris*

In Japan: Please write to *Longman Penguin Japan Co Ltd, Yamaguchi Building, 2–12–9 Kanda Jimbocho, Chiyoda-Ku, Tokyo 101*

FOR THE BEST IN PAPERBACKS, LOOK FOR THE 🐧

PENGUIN HEALTH

Audrey Eyton's F-Plus   Audrey Eyton

'Your short cut to the most sensational diet of the century' – *Daily Express*

Baby and Child   Penelope Leach

A beautifully illustrated and comprehensive handbook on the first five years of life. 'It stands head and shoulders above anything else available at the moment' – Mary Kenny in the *Spectator*

Woman's Experience of Sex   Sheila Kitzinger

Fully illustrated with photographs and line drawings, this book explores the riches of women's sexuality at every stage of life. 'A book which any mother could confidently pass on to her daughter – and her partner too' – *Sunday Times*

Food Additives   Erik Millstone

Eat, drink and be worried? Erik Millstone's hard-hitting book contains powerful evidence about the massive risks being taken with the health of the consumer. It takes the lid off food and the food industry.

Living with Allergies   Dr John McKenzie

At least 20% of the population suffer from an allergic disorder at some point in their lives and this invaluable book provides accurate and up-to-date information about the condition, where to go for help, diagnosis and cure – and what we can do to help ourselves.

Living with Stress   Cary L. Cooper, Rachel D. Cooper and Lynn H. Eaker

Stress leads to more stress, and the authors of this helpful book show why low levels of stress are desirable and how best we can achieve them in today's world. Looking at those most vulnerable, they demonstrate ways of breaking the vicious circle that can ruin lives.

FOR THE BEST IN PAPERBACKS, LOOK FOR THE

PENGUIN HEALTH

Living with Asthma and Hay Fever   John Donaldson

For the first time, there are now medicines that can prevent asthma attacks from taking place. Based on up-to-date research, this book shows how the majority of sufferers can beat asthma and hay fever and lead full and active lives.

Anorexia Nervosa   R. L. Palmer

Lucid and sympathetic guidance for those who suffer from this disturbing illness, and for their families and professional helpers, given with a clarity and compassion that will make anorexia more understandable and consequently less frightening for everyone involved.

Medicines: A Guide for Everybody   Peter Parish

This sixth edition of a comprehensive survey of all the medicines available over the counter or on prescription offers clear guidance for the ordinary reader as well as invaluable information for those involved in health care.

Pregnancy and Childbirth   Sheila Kitzinger

A complete and up-to-date guide to physical and emotional preparation for pregnancy – a must for all prospective parents.

The Penguin Encyclopaedia of Nutrition   John Yudkin

This book cuts through all the myths about food and diets to present the real facts clearly and simply. 'Everyone should buy one' – *Nutrition News and Notes*

The Parents' A to Z   Penelope Leach

For anyone with children of 6 months, 6 years or 16 years, this guide to all the little problems involved in their health, growth and happiness will prove reassuring and helpful.

PENGUIN HEALTH

Positive Smear   Susan Quilliam

A 'positive' cervical smear result is not only a medical event but an emotional event too: one which means facing up to issues surrounding your sexuality, fertility and mortality. Based on personal experiences, Susan Quilliam's practical guide will help every woman meet that challenge.

Medicine   The Self-Help Guide
Professor Michael Orme and Dr Susanna Grahame-Jones

A new kind of home doctor – with an entirely new approach. With a unique emphasis on self-management, *Medicine* takes an *active* approach to drugs, showing how to maximize their benefits, speed up recovery and minimize dosages through self-help and non-drug alternatives.

Defeating Depression   Tony Lake

Counselling, medication and the support of friends can all provide invaluable help in relieving depression. But if we are to combat it once and for all we must face up to perhaps painful truths about our past and take the first steps forward that can eventually transform our lives. This lucid and sensitive book shows us how.

Freedom and Choice in Childbirth   Sheila Kitzinger

Undogmatic, honest and compassionate, Sheila Kitzinger's book raises searching questions about the kind of care offered to the pregnant woman – and will help her make decisions and communicate effectively about the kind of birth experience she desires.

Care of the Dying   Richard Lamerton

It is never true that 'nothing more can be done' for the dying. This book shows us how to face death without pain, with humanity, with dignity and in peace.

PENGUIN LITERARY CRITICISM

Modernism Malcolm Bradbury and James McFarlane (eds.)

A brilliant collection of essays dealing with every aspect of literature and culture during the period 1890–1930 – from Apollinaire and Brecht to Yeats and Zola.

The New Pelican Guide to English Literature Boris Ford (ed.)

The indispensable critical guide to English literature in eight volumes, erudite yet accessible. From the ages of Chaucer and Shakespeare, via Georgian satirists and Victorian social critics, to the leading writers of the 1980s, all literary life is here.

The Theatre of the Absurd Martin Esslin

This classic study of the dramatists of the Absurd examines the origins, nature and future of a movement whose significance has transcended the bounds of the stage and influenced the whole intellectual climate of our time.

The Theory of the Modern Stage Eric Bentley (ed.)

In this anthology Artaud, Brecht, Stanislavski and other great theatrical theorists reveal the ideas underlying their productions and point to the possibilities of the modern theatre.

Introducing Shakespeare G. B. Harrison

An excellent popular introduction to Shakespeare – the legend, the (tantalizingly ill-recorded) life and the work – in the context of his times: theatrical rivalry, literary piracy, the famous performance of *Richard II* in support of Essex, and the fire which finally destroyed the Globe.

Aspects of the Novel E. M. Forster

'I say that I have never met this kind of perspicacity in literary criticism before. I could quote scores of examples of startling excellence' – Arnold Bennett. Originating in a course of lectures given at Cambridge, *Aspects of the Novel* is full of E. M. Forster's habitual wit, wisdom and freshness of approach.

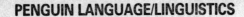